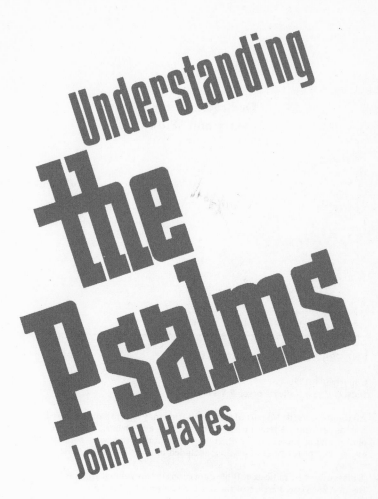

Understanding the Psalms

John H. Hayes

Judson Press • Valley Forge

Dedicated to my in-laws
Mary and Wilton Hall

UNDERSTANDING THE PSALMS

Copyright © 1976
Judson Press, Valley Forge, PA 19481

Library of Congress Cataloging in Publication Data
Hayes, John Haralson, 1934-
  Understanding the Psalms.

  1. Bible. O.T. Psalms—Introductions. I. Title.
BS1430.2.H35   223'.2'06   75-22034
ISBN 0-8170-0683-4

Printed in the U.S.A.

Contents

General Introduction

Throughout the centuries, the book of Psalms has nurtured the life and faith of Jews in their synagogues and Christians in their churches. Through their use of the Psalms, Judaism and Christianity have given expression to their prayers and have listened to the voice of their God.

The great German reformer, Martin Luther, in speaking of the book of Psalms, declared that "the Psalter is the favourite book of all the saints." In explaining why this is the case, Luther's comments could hardly be improved: "[Each person], whatever his circumstances may be, finds in [the book] psalms and words which are appropriate to the circumstances in which he finds himself and meet his needs as adequately as if they were composed exclusively for his sake, and in such a way that he himself could not improve on them nor could find or desire any better psalms or words." [1]

In the Psalter, one finds psalms expressive of the gamut of human emotions. Some ring with the exuberant thrill of praise; others reverberate with the throes of human desperation. The heights and the depths of human life resound through its poetry.

The unashamed proclamation of adulation peels through some psalms, as in the following call for an orchestrated praise of God.

> Praise the Lord!
> Praise God in his sanctuary;
> praise him in his mighty firmament!
> Praise him for his mighty deeds;
> praise him according to his exceeding greatness!

[1] Quoted in Artur Weiser, *The Psalms* (Philadelphia: The Westminster Press, 1962), p. 20.

Praise him with trumpet sound;
    praise him with lute and harp!
Praise him with timbrel and dance;
    praise him with strings and pipe!
Praise him with sounding cymbals;
    praise him with loud clashing cymbals!
Let everything that breathes praise the Lord!
Praise the Lord!

(Psalm 150)

Some psalms speak of the reassuring comfort of the divine presence and protection.

The Lord is my shepherd, I shall not want;
    he makes me lie down in green pastures.
He leads me beside still waters;
    he restores my soul.
He leads me in paths of righteousness
    for his name's sake.
Even though I walk through the valley of the shadow of death,
    I fear no evil;
for thou art with me;
    thy rod and thy staff, they comfort me.

(Psalm 23:1-4)

Elsewhere, the sense of abject estrangement from God—the absence of the divine presence—permeates the prayer of pathos.

My God, my God, why hast thou forsaken me?
    Why art thou so far from helping me, from the words of my
        groaning?
O my God, I cry by day, but thou dost not answer;
    and by night, but find no rest.

(Psalm 22:1-2)

The expression of overbearing sin characterizes many of the psalms.

For I know my transgressions,
    and my sin is ever before me.
Against thee, thee only, have I sinned,
    and done that which is evil in thy sight,
so that thou art justified in thy sentence
    and blameless in thy judgment.

> Behold, I was brought forth in iniquity,
> and in sin did my mother conceive me.
> (Psalm 51:3-5)

Such a feeling of sin and unworthiness calls forth a plea for forgiveness and restoration.

> Purge me with hyssop, and I shall be clean;
> wash me, and I shall be whiter than snow.
> Fill me with joy and gladness;
> let the bones which thou hast broken rejoice.
> Hide thy face from my sins,
> and blot out all my iniquities.
> Create in me a clean heart, O God,
> and put a new and right spirit within me.
> (Psalm 51:7-10)

Other psalms contain no hint of a confession of sin; in fact, the psalmist affirms his innocence in unequivocal terms.

> Prove me, O Lord, and try me;
> test my heart and my mind.
> For thy steadfast love is before my eyes,
> and I walk in faithfulness to thee.
> I do not sit with false men,
> nor do I consort with dissemblers;
> I hate the company of evildoers,
> and I will not sit with the wicked.
> But as for me, I walk in my integrity. . . .
> My foot stands on level ground. . . .
> (Psalm 26:2-5, 11-12)

The sense of sin and the threat of judgment are not the only sentiments in the psalms which express the psalmists' desperation. There are psalms which speak of menacing enemies, disloyal friends, debilitating sickness, workers of iniquity, and death itself, which threaten a person's life and faith.

In some psalms it is God himself who is depicted as the enemy, as the cause of grief. The psalms claim that God is expressing his enmity though there is no human condition that would justify such a divine attitude.

> Yet thou hast cast us off and abased us,
> and hast not gone out with our armies.

Thou hast made us turn back from the foe;
    and our enemies have gotten spoil.
All this has come upon us,
    though we have not forgotten thee,
    or been false to thy covenant.
                                (Psalm 44:9-10, 17)

Many psalms are saturated with hatred and vitriolic pleading for vengeance upon an enemy. The worst of human predicaments are called down upon the head of an opponent.

When he is tried, let him come forth guilty;
    let his prayer be counted as sin!
May his days be few:
    may another seize his goods!
May his children be fatherless,
    and his wife a widow!
May his children wander about and beg;
    may they be driven out of the ruins they inhabit!
                                (Psalm 109:7-10)

This is piety tinged with hatred. Or is it hatred tinged with piety?

This gamut of human emotions—or as Luther said, these words "appropriate to the circumstances"—appears in the psalms not only in the sentiments of individuals but also the expressions of the community.

How can we best examine the psalms in order to understand, appreciate, and identify with this gamut of human emotions? We should note first of all the great similarity and diversity within the Psalter.

SIMILARITY AND DIVERSITY IN THE PSALMS

When one sits down and quickly reads through the book of Psalms, one is generally struck by two contradictory impressions. On the one hand, the reader encounters a great diversity in the material. The book contains no unifying plot, no continuous narrative, and no central theme which binds all the individual units together. The interests and subject matter of the psalms focus on a wide range of topics. On the other hand, the reader can note a striking similarity between many of the psalms and at points may begin to wonder if he or she is not rereading earlier passages. Ideas, expressions, and concerns reappear in different psalms throughout the book. Many of the psalms tend to open or close with almost identical phraseology.

This simultaneous sense of both diversity and similarity in the psalms is not due to the reader's failure to understand the material nor to lack of attention to details in the text. It is inherent in the nature of the book of Psalms.

How is this diversity and similarity to be explained and understood? Must it be overcome in order to arrive at an appreciation of the psalms?

In a way, the diversity and similarity in the psalms provide the key for interpreting and understanding them. The similarity between various psalms allows us to divide the psalms into various types, according to their content, mood, expressions, and structure. Grouping the psalms into categories or types according to their similarities provides the reader with a framework within which the psalms can be analyzed and studied according to their organic typology.

Once the psalms can be recognized to fall into common types, the student of the psalms can confront the issue of the diversity in the book of Psalms. Why are there numerous psalms, on the one hand, characterized by a mood of mourning, almost desperation, and, on the other hand, numerous psalms characterized by a mood of joy and a sense of celebration? Why are there many psalms which focus on the individual worshiper and other psalms concerned with the interests of the community at large? Why are there numerous psalms which praise the deity and other psalms which implore the deity to act or come close to blaming the deity for inactivity? This diversity among the categories of psalms is to be understood in terms of the reasons lying behind the purposes for which the psalms were written and the occasions on which they were used.

THE VARIOUS TYPES OF PSALMS

The most common type of psalm in the Bible is concerned with the distress of an individual who addresses the deity, asking that he be saved from some predicament. A typical example of this class is Psalm 17. In this psalm, the individual describes the wicked enemies who surround him, speaking arrogantly and desiring to attack him like a lion from ambush (Psalm 17:10-12). He prays that God would overthrow his enemies and deliver him from his opponents (Psalm 17:13-14).

Another group of psalms, closely akin to the preceding, has the individual looking back upon the distress from which he has been saved and offering thanks for his redemption. Psalm 30 presents a good example of this type of psalm. In this psalm, reference is made to the previous distress in which the man found himself (Psalm 30:3, 11), to the prayers he prayed in his time of trouble (Psalm 30:2, 8-10), and to the thanksgiving he now offers for his salvation (Psalm 30:1, 4-5, 11-12).

The psalm of individual distress and the psalm of individual thanksgiving represent the two basic attitudes which a person may take toward personal troubles and the predicaments of distress. They reflect the two basic forms of addressing the deity, petition and praise. In the psalm of distress, the distress is experienced as a personal, engulfing, life-threatening reality and the deity is implored and petitioned to act on behalf of the distressed individual. The psalm laments the present condition of existence and looks forward in hope to a better time and improved conditions. The psalm of thanksgiving, on the other hand, looks back upon the situation of distress as a past reality from which redemption has been experienced, and God is praised for his action of salvation which has changed the life and fate of the one praying. In both types of psalms there is frequently a call to other persons to share in and learn from the experience and faith of the one praying (see Psalm 30:4-5).

A third class of psalms, in addition to psalms of personal distress and individual thanksgiving, is a group of psalms whose concern is a situation of distress or calamity involving the community as a whole. Psalm 74 is an example of this type. In this psalm, the enemies of the people have destroyed the sanctuary of God and there is no prophet to say how long the destruction will last (vv. 1-11). The community, after expressing its faith in God (vv. 12-17), requests that God remember his covenant people and take vengeance on its adversaries (vv. 20-23).

Just as the individual psalm of thanksgiving is the counterpart to the individual psalm of distress, so the communal psalm of thanksgiving is the counterpart to the communal psalm of distress. For some reason, however, very few psalms which express the thanksgiving of the community are to be found in the book of Psalms. An example of this type is Psalm 124 which confesses that, had it not been for God, the people would have been swallowed in a flood of raging waters.

A fifth class of psalms may be designated as hymns. Psalms in this group are similar in their intent and content; they are all psalms which praise God. Psalm 29 is a typical example.

Many psalms which belong to the category of hymns or songs of praise do not have God as the primary object of praise. For example, Psalm 45 is a psalm in praise of the king and his bride on their wedding day. Thus one could classify this and other such psalms as royal hymns. Psalm 48 is a song in praise of God, but its basic concern is to extol the greatness of Zion. This praise of Zion—another name for Jerusalem—is even more obvious in Psalm 87. Thus it is proper to speak of Zion songs, which have a clear focus of concern centered on the Holy City of Jerusalem.

There are numerous psalms which defy a simple classification. They are neither psalms of distress or thanksgiving nor are they hymns of praise. If we take an obvious example and analyze its structure and content, this will become quite clear. Psalm 24 contains the following parts:

A. (1-2): Hymn in praise of God
B. (3):   Question about ascending the hill of the Lord
C. (4-5): Answer
D. (6):   Response to the answer
E. (7):   Address to the gates
F. (8):   Question and response
G. (9):   Address to the gates
H. (10): Question and response

The elements in this psalm clearly have no parallel to the other psalms we have noted. How can one classify such a psalm as this on the basis of its structure and content? The structure of the psalm suggests a litany, a liturgy in which various persons or groups participated.

Now let us summarize the discussion to this point. We have noted that the vast majority of the psalms can be placed into five major classifications. Many psalms appeal to the deity for salvation from the midst of a situation of distress. Sometimes it is an individual person; at other times it is the community which is undergoing trouble and crisis. Other psalms—both individual and communal—offer thanks to the deity and look back upon the distress and crisis as a thing of the past. Other psalms are unrelated to any situation of distress but instead are psalms of praise—praising God, the king, Zion, or something else sacred such as the law (see Psalm 19:7-10). Other psalms defy a straightforward classification: many of these are characterized by elements best seen as parts of litanies or liturgies.

The questions that we must now ask in attempting to understand the psalms are the following: Why were the psalms written? Do the various classifications of the psalms give any indication as to why they were written? How were the psalms employed in ancient Israel? Can we associate the psalms with actual life situations in which they would have been utilized?

THE PSALMS AND WORSHIP

Many factors both within and outside the psalms point to services of worship as the arena within which the psalms were originally employed and for which they were composed.

1. Many psalms contain references to participation in worship or cultic events. Psalm 5:7 speaks of entering God's house and worshiping toward his holy temple. Psalm 122:1 refers to the joy of making a journey to the temple. In Psalm 26:6-7 the speaker talks of washing his hands in innocence, going about the altar, singing aloud a song of thanksgiving, and testifying to God's wondrous deeds. The procession into the sanctuary accompanied by singers and minstrels is referred to in Psalm 68:24-27, and the worshiper's participation in such a procession is noted in Psalm 42:4.

2. The psalms contain numerous references to the temple and ritual acts. Allusions and references to the temple, Mount Zion, the sacred city, and sacrifices in the psalms are too numerous to note. All of these, however, clearly point toward the use of the psalms in cultic worship. Many of the psalms were no doubt spoken as the oral accompaniment to the ritual to which reference is made.

3. The frequent references in the psalms to musical instruments of diverse types, to singing, and to dancing point to religious activities. Many of the psalms are designated as "songs" in their titles, which frequently note that the psalm is to be accompanied with stringed instruments (see Psalm 67).

4. The direct address of prayers to God, the admonition to others to join in the praise or thanksgiving, the speeches of God, and the structure of the psalms are all best understood in terms of activities associated with worship.

5. In the narrative books of the Old Testament, a few references are made to the employment of psalms within the context of worship. After Hannah had prayed in the temple for a child (1 Samuel 1:10-11), she conceived, and after the child was weaned, she presented him to the temple. She and her family then worshiped, and she is depicted as reciting a prayer—a psalm—on that occasion (1 Samuel 2:1-10). First Chronicles 16 narrates the story of David's transference of the ark to Jerusalem. On that occasion, the text states that Asaph and his

brethren—a group of temple singers—sang psalms (Psalms 105:1-15; 96:1-13; and 106:1, 47-48 are quoted). At the rededication of the walls of Jerusalem under Nehemiah, we are told that Levites came to aid in the celebration, "with thanksgivings and singing, with cymbals, harps, and lyres" (Nehemiah 12:27). After King Hezekiah had recovered from his sickness, he is said to have composed a writing (Isaiah 38:9-20). This poem of Hezekiah, related to the time after his recovery, is a typical psalm of individual thanksgiving, comparable to the type noted above. These references associate the use of psalms with services of worship and support the idea that the psalms were employed on diverse occasions in cultic worship.

ISRAELITE WORSHIP

If the psalms were originally related to the worship services of ancient Israel, we need to understand the nature and character of Israelite worship in order to understand how the psalms were employed in that worship. Numerous Old Testament passages allow us to reconstruct at least the general outline of worship in ancient Israel, although there are many issues about which we have little or no information. First of all, let us examine the material related to those religious activities which focus on the individual.

When we think of services of worship which focus on the individual in contemporary culture, infant dedications or baptisms, confirmations, weddings, and funerals immediately come to mind. In ancient Israel there were no religious or cultic services comparable to these. Circumcisions, weddings, and burial services were certainly observed, but these were "secular" events in that they were not activities performed in a place of worship.

Examination of Old Testament texts reveals five areas in which cultic activities which centered on the individual were performed. One of these was concerned with the individual's fulfillment of certain religious obligations, such as offering the first fruits from his field and the payment of tithes to the temple. Deuteronomy 26:1-11 outlines the ritual involved when a man brought the first fruits of his field to the sanctuary. After harvesting his crops, portions of these were taken, placed in a basket, and carried to the temple where they were presented to God. In a ritual presided over by a priest, the presentation of the produce was made and the worshiper testified to his faith by repeating a confession summarizing God's great events performed in Israel's sacred history. He then worshiped the Lord and rejoiced in the good which God had given him. When tithes were presented, the person swore before the Lord that he had fulfilled all the obligations and regulations concerning his offering (Deuteronomy 26:12-15).

A second area of cultic concern centered on the individual was related to times of illness and disease. Many of the actions of the individual related to certain diseases are discussed in Leviticus 13–15. The regulations in these chapters only deal with special illnesses—leprosy and certain diseases which produced discharges. Leprosy in the Old Testament refers to a wide range of skin diseases, and even cloth and houses could be plagued with "leprosy," that is, with some type of fungus growth. Because of their contagious character, the handling of these types of disease was carefully regulated. When a man had a suspicious skin affliction, he had to present himself for examination by the priests who declared him either clean or unclean. If a man was declared unclean, that is, if he possessed an abnormal condition, then he was required to tear his clothes, to let his hair hang loose, to cover his mouth, to cry out "unclean, unclean" as he went about, and to live apart from the community (Leviticus 13:1-46). This ostracism from family, community, and ordinary life is painfully reflected in one of Job's laments about his condition (see Job 19:13-22).

When a man's disease showed signs of healing, he was reexamined by a priest, and if he had healed, certain rituals performed over a period of eight days reintegrated him into the community and effected atonement with God. These rituals involved the killing of a bird over running water, the use of cedarwood, scarlet cloth, and hyssop (a small herb), and applying the blood of the killed bird to the man and to another bird which was released alive. The man was required to bathe, shave his body, wash his clothes, and live isolated for seven more days. On the eighth day he offered special sacrifices at the temple, had his right earlobe, right thumb, and right big toe smeared with sacrificial blood and oil, and was declared clean and purified (Leviticus 14:1-32). Similar but not identical rituals were performed when bodily discharges existed (Leviticus 15).

Although the laws in Leviticus do not refer to these, it may be assumed that prayers—psalms—were offered by ill persons on the occasion of their sickness and purification and probably not just when illnesses rendering one unclean were involved. As we shall see, many individual psalms of distress and thanksgiving are concerned with sickness of various sorts.

Special legal procedures provided a third set of circumstances in which the individual was brought into special relationship to the cult. Hebrew law distinguished between murder and manslaughter and provided special regulations by which the person guilty of manslaughter could escape the revenge of the murdered man's nearest of kin and tribal relatives. Exodus 21:12-14 provides for this circumstance and stipulates that the right of asylum must be granted the man guilty of manslaughter. Other passages, such as Deuteronomy 19:1-13; 1 Kings 1:49-53; and 1 Kings 2:28-35, associate this right to asylum, even where killing was not involved, with seeking refuge in the sanctuary. The life of the manslaughterer was placed in great jeopardy even though he had killed accidently. In seeking refuge and asylum in the temple, a man saved his life, but his liberty was forfeited and his family relationships severed. He was now to live by the mercy and grace of God. Several psalms speak of seeking refuge in God and no doubt have this practice of asylum as their background.

Ordinary court cases were tried within the city gate in Israel. When special circumstances—lack of evidence or witnesses—made it impossible for the elders to decide a case, special procedures involving the parties took place at the temple. Exodus 22:7-8; Deuteronomy 17:8-13; 19:15-21; 1 Kings 8:31-32; and Numbers 5:5-31 provide some clues as to what went on. The parties, or at least the accused, had to take an oath of innocence and rely upon the verdict of God (see especially 1 Kings 8:31-32). Numbers 5:5-31 outlines the ritual of ordeal undertaken by a woman when accused of adultery by her husband. The woman was required to take an oath or self-curse and to drink a concoction composed of holy water, dust swept from the floor of the sanctuary, and the written curses washed into the drink. In addition, she had to offer a sacrifice. Joshua 7 and 1 Samuel 14:24-46 note that, in some cases, guilt was determined by the casting of lots. As we shall see, several of the individual psalms of distress envisioned charges being brought against the one pleading his or her case and seem to have these legal practices at the sanctuary as their setting.

When a person was guilty of sin, special activities were carried out by that person at the sanctuary in order to find atonement with God. These services provided the fourth situation in which worship concentrated on the individual. Leviticus 4:1–6:7 discusses some of the circumstances associated with these rituals of personal atonement. Failure to offer testimony in court, touching an unclean thing, making rash oaths, breach of faith, deceiving one's neighbor, and swearing falsely are among the sins noted in this material. To rectify the sinful state, the guilty had to confess their sin, make restitution to the injured party where injury was involved, and offer sacrifice for atonement. Several psalms are concerned with committed sins and the desire or thanksgiving for forgiveness and should no doubt be seen within the context of the rituals outlined in Leviticus 4:1–6:7.

A fifth complex of occasions involving the individual worshiper concerned the fulfillment of special vows that a person might make (see Genesis 28:18-22; 2 Samuel 15:7-9) or the presentation of special offerings (freewill sacrifices; see Leviticus 7:16) that a person might wish to present to God.

The primary worship services in ancient Israel were community affairs. Regular and routine services were held daily, on the sabbath, at the new moon (first day of the month), and at seasonal festivals. References to the daily sacrifices are noted in Exodus 29:38-46; Numbers 28:1-8; 1 Kings 18:36; and 2 Kings 16:15. Although the Old Testament itself does not refer to the singing of psalms in conjunction with daily sacrifices, we know from later Jewish tradition that the following psalms were sung during the daily services: Psalm 24 (Sunday); Psalm 48 (Monday); Psalm 82 (Tuesday); Psalm 94 (Wednesday); Psalm 81 (Thursday); Psalm 93 (Friday); and Psalm 92 (Saturday; see the title to Psalm 92). This selection of psalms for the daily services reflects the practice during the time of the second temple, but on the basis of this evidence it can be concluded that such a use of some psalms was quite ancient. On the sabbath, double the daily sacrifices were offered (see Numbers 28:9-10 and note the precautions taken at the temple on the sabbath, perhaps due to the large crowds in attendance, in the story recorded in 2 Kings 11). New moon services are noted in the Old Testament, but we know very little about what occurred during these services (see Numbers 10:10; 28:11-15; 1 Samuel 20:5; 2 Kings 4:23; Hosea 2:11).

The basic festivals of early Israel, at which attendance at the sanctuary by all males was required, were the Feasts of Unleavened Bread, Harvest (also known as Feast of Weeks or Pentecost), and Ingathering (also known as Feast of Booths or Tabernacles). All of these festivals were associated with the agricultural season. To appreciate properly the importance of the seasonal associations of these festivals, it is necessary to comment briefly on the climatic conditions of Palestine. The area is characterized by two dominant seasons. The wet and winter season began about October with the first rains, after which cereal crops (barley and wheat) were planted.

The winter season was therefore a time of growth. The rainy season ceased about April, after which the grains were harvested—first barley and then wheat. The summer crops—grapes, olives, and fruits—ripened during the rainless summer months. These were gathered in before the first rains in the fall.

The Old Testament contains a number of passages which discuss these three festivals (Exodus 23:14-17; 34:18-26; Leviticus 23; Deuteronomy 16:1-17). The earliest festival in the spring was the Feast of Unleavened Bread which was observed for seven days in the month of Abib (later, this month was called Nisan), which corresponds roughly to late March and early April. At the time of this festival, all the leavened food had to be thrown out and all leaven (yeast) removed from the homes. For a week, the newly harvested barley was eaten without being leavened. Since bread was probably leavened by mixing a yeast plug from the previous batch of dough (just as our grandmothers did!), the removal of the leaven meant that the yeast plug could not be carried over and mixed with the new crop. The eating of unleavened bread provided a dramatic portrayal of the end of the old harvest period and the beginning of the new. It was what sociologists call a "rite of passage," that is, a ritual which marks the movement from one status, time, or condition to another. (One can compare the events associated with college graduation to see how we still preserve rites of passage and how traditional their forms are.)

The oldest passages on the calendars of worship in Israel (Exodus 23 and 34) do not associate the Feast of Passover with the Feast of Unleavened Bread, as later became the case. Passover (see Exodus 12) seems not to have originally been an agricultural observance. It was a shepherds' festival, involving the slaughter of a lamb, the eating of the cooked lamb at night, and the smearing of the doorposts or tentposts with blood. This observance, which was held in the early spring, was probably originally a festival held on the night before shepherds left their winter grazing lands to begin migrating to their summer pastures. Its intent was, no doubt, to protect the flocks, new lambs, and shepherds in the subsequent change of pastures. Note that Exodus 12:23 refers to "the destroyer" who would be warded off by the protective blood. Passover was, therefore, originally a festival celebrated "at home," away from the sanctuary, prior to moving to a "new home."

A number of factors led to the eventual association of Passover and Unleavened Bread. They both occurred about the same time of the year—about the middle of the first spring month. Both emphasized the eating of unleavened bread—the Feast of Un-leavened Bread stressing the change of seasons and Passover noting the ordinary bread of nomads and shepherds which was and still is prepared without yeast. Both festivals came to commemorate the Exodus from Egypt (see Exodus 12 on Passover and Exodus 23:15 on the Feast of Unleavened Bread). By the time Deuteronomy was written, probably in the seventh century B.C., Passover had become a festival associated with the Feast of Unleavened Bread and had to be observed in Jerusalem (Deuteronomy 16:1-8).

The emphases of Passover-Unleavened Bread were, therefore, two-fold. On the one hand, there was the emphasis on the harvest and new crops. On the other hand, there was stress on the great redemption experienced in the Exodus from Egypt. In the obser-vances in the temple and at the Passover meal, these two interests were given expression in word and deed.

A second major festival in Israel was the Feast of Harvest (Weeks or Pentecost), held seven weeks after the beginning of the barley harvest. This festival, one day in length, coincided with the wheat harvest. It thus closed the season of harvest associated with the cereal crops. Here, too, the focus on the harvest was a special emphasis.

The spring complex of celebrations—Passover-Unleavened Bread-Pentecost—were all festivals of joyous celebrations com-memorating the Exodus experience and offering thanksgiving for the new harvest. Numerous psalms—many hymns of praise—focus on Israel's Exodus from Egypt, her possession of the land of Canaan, and God's care of and gifts to his people. These psalms, in other words, give expression to the central themes of the spring celebrations and no doubt were used in these celebrations.

The third major festival in Israel was celebrated in the fall, during the seventh month, which corresponds to late September and early October. This festival, called the Feast of Ingathering, Booths, or Tabernacles, was held after the harvest of fruits, olives, and grapes. It also occurred at the season just prior to the beginning of the autumn rains and the sowing of the new crops. Exodus 23:16 dates this festival "at the end of the year." Thus it marked the transition from the old year to the new. In the oldest calendars, no definite date or length is stipulated for the festival. In the later calendar, the feast was to be celebrated for seven days.

The fullest discussion of the fall festival complex is found in Leviticus 23:23-43. This passage, which probably dates from after the fall of Jerusalem in 586 B.C., set the pattern which was and still is observed in Judaism. Here there are three elements or three successive celebrations: the Memorial of New Year's Day (Rosh Hashanah) on the first day of the seventh month, the Day of Atonement (Yom Kippur) on the tenth day, and the Feast of Booths from the fifteenth until the twenty-second. The New Year's Day was a time of solemn rest. The Day of Atonement (see Leviticus 16) was a day of penitence with fasting, self-affliction, and rituals centered on the forgiveness of communal and national guilt. A primary ritual of the Day of Atonement was the release of the scapegoat in the wilderness. The goat carried away the sins of the people. Special convocations were held during the Feast of Booths.

What themes were celebrated in the fall complex of festivities? Obviously, a basic element centered on national guilt and forgiveness as is evidenced in the rituals of the first and tenth days. In later Judaism we know that the new year's celebration was associated with the idea of the creation of the world. About the only passage, outside of the Old Testament law books, which mentions the Feast of Booths is Zechariah 14:16-21. In this passage, the emphasis in the feast falls on the celebration of the Israelite God as king of the world. In addition, rain is promised for those who participate in the festival. The fall festival therefore focused on the guilt and atonement of the people, celebrated the creative work of God and his universal kingship, and anticipated the coming agricultural year and, in paricular, the life-giving autumn rains on which the entire fabric of Israelite life was so dependent. Numerous psalms celebrate God's creation of the world, his reign as king over Israel and the nations, and proclaim judgment and forgiveness for Israel. These psalms are best understood in light of their employment in the celebration of the fall festivals.

In addition to the daily, weekly, monthly, and seasonal communal celebrations in ancient Israel, we should note one other set of celebrations by the community. These involved events in which the king and his rule were the central concerns. The king in Jerusalem was an individual, but he was more than this. He was the representative and the embodiment of the community. The central routine ritual associated with the king was, of course, his coronation. On the basis of 1 Kings 1 and 2 Kings 11, the ritual of the coronation can be partially reconstructed; and on the basis of this reconstruction, it is possible to see how many of the royal psalms fit within this celebration of the community.

In addition to the regular, recurring, routine communal celebrations, special services were held when the community's life and welfare were threatened. Special services were held at the time of military conflict both before and after battle. During times of drought and famine, special observances involving fasts and prayers for deliverance were held (see 1 Kings 8:33-53 and the Book of Joel). Many of the communal psalms of distress belong within this context. Communal psalms of thanksgiving would have been offered after the passing of the distress.

In subsequent chapters we shall examine the various types of psalms in terms of their usage within these services of individual and public worship which we have outlined in this chapter.

Hymns of Praise

Human address to the divine expresses itself in two basic modes: petition and praise. In praise, the worshiping individual or community offers adoration to the deity and proclaims his magnificence and the greatness of his works and deeds. In singing hymns of praise, the congregation feels itself in the glorious and holy presence of God and extols what God is and does for the community. In praising God, the mood of the hymn reflects reverence, laudation, and enthusiasm. Emotional fervor gives expression to what the community senses, feels, and believes as it offers its praise to God and proclaims his greatness to men.

THE STRUCTURE OF THE HYMN

Examples of hymns of praise in the Psalter are Psalms 8; 29; 47; 93; 95–100; 104; 113–115; 117; 135–136; 146–150. Many other psalms contain sections or verses which are praises of God. In addition, some of the hymns of general thanksgiving may be considered as praises of God (see Psalms 67; 103; 105–107; 111; 124).

Most of the hymns of praise share characteristic features and a common structural pattern. The structure is comprised of three elements: the introductory exhortation or call to praise, the main body of the hymn which praises God for his attributes and deeds, and a concluding section expressing some wish, prayer, or blessing.

The introductory exhortation is a call to worship, praise, thank, or bless God. It is addressed to those who are called to share in the worship or praise. This exhortation employs a wide variety of expressions, both in the manner in which it speaks of praising God and in regard to those who are called upon to praise him. Some examples will illustrate this:

> Ascribe to the Lord, O heavenly beings,
>   ascribe to the Lord glory and strength.
> Ascribe to the Lord the glory of his name;
>   worship the Lord in holy array.
>   (Psalm 29:1-2)

> Clap your hands, all peoples!
> Shout to God with loud songs of joy!
>   (Psalm 47:1)

> O come, let us sing to the Lord;
>   let us make a joyful noise to the rock of our salvation!
> Let us come into his presence with thanksgiving;
>   let us make a joyful noise to him with songs of praise!
>   (Psalm 95:1-2)

> O sing to the Lord a new song;
>   sing to the Lord, all the earth!
> Sing to the Lord, bless his name;
>   tell of his salvation from day to day.
>   (Psalm 96:1-2)

> Praise the Lord!
> Praise, O servants of the Lord,
>   praise the name of the Lord!
>   (Psalm 113:1)

> Not to us, O Lord, not to us,
>   but to thy name give glory. . . .
>   (Psalm 115:1)

> Praise the Lord!
> Praise the Lord from the heavens,
>   praise him in the heights!
> Praise him, all his angels,
>   praise him, all his hosts!
> Praise him, sun and moon,
>   praise him, all you shining stars!
> Praise him, you highest heavens,
>   and you waters above the heavens!
>   (Psalm 148:1-4)

The diversity of those who are addressed and invited to praise in these calls to worship is truly astounding! Sometimes the psalmist calls upon his soul to praise God. At other times it is the nation

Israel, the sons of Zion, or the servants of God. The world at large and the nations are summoned. Sometimes it is the heavenly beings, the angels, who are called upon to praise God (see Isaiah 6:1-3). At other times the created elements or all creation are beckoned to offer praise. One hymn (Psalm 115) seems to call upon God to offer praise to himself or his name. Psalm 148 is by far the most inclusive in its enumeration of those who should offer praise: angels, sun and moon, shining stars and highest heavens, sea monsters and the deep, mountains and hills, fruit trees and cedars, creeping things and flying birds, kings and princes, men and maidens, old and young. The psalmist here envisions the whole of the universe as one massive chorus offering to God his rightful praise.

The exuberance of the psalmists' desire to give expression to the need for praise thus encompasses not only the Chosen People of Israel but also the whole of the created order. One must certainly see here the jubilation of the community which wishes to express itself in the widest possible sense. So great is the feeling of praise that inanimate objects, foreign peoples, and the heavenly powers are metaphorically enlisted in the great cantatas of praise. The psalmists seem to say that not only men and women but also the whole universe must sing for joy if God is to know the true praise which he so richly deserves.

Many of the expressive acts which were part of the experience of praise are referred to in these psalms. The accompaniment of musical instruments, the singing of songs, the clapping of hands, making melody, and dancing are noted explicitly. The ancient Israelite community was not ashamed nor hesitant to give full range to its praise and to express its jubilant celebration. When one worshiped such a God as Israel's God, praise must be unlimited, as wide as the heavens and as boundless as the sea!

The main body of the psalm contains the actual proclamation of divine praise. This section is, of course, the center and heart of the hymn of praise. It gives expression to the basis for praising God. Two important factors should be noted about this element of the psalm. In the first place, there seem to be two basic ways in which this praise was expressed: God may, in the first place, be praised in general terms which enumerate his lasting qualities or glorify his mighty deeds or, secondly, the hymn may focus on some special attribute of the divine or some single event of redemptive activity.

An example of the first of these is Psalm 136. The psalm praises God

. . . who alone does great wonders . . .
    who by understanding made the heavens;
        who spread out the earth upon the waters;
            who made the great lights,
                the sun to rule over the day,
                    the moon and stars to rule over the night.
Who smote the first-born of Egypt
    and brought Israel out from among them
        with a strong hand and an outstretched arm;
who divided the Red Sea in sunder
    and made Israel pass through the midst of it,
        but overthrew Pharaoh and his host in the Red Sea.
Who led his people through the wilderness;
    who smote great kings,
        and slew famous kings,
            and gave their land as a heritage,
                a heritage to Israel his servant.
Who remembered us in our low estate,
    and rescued us from our foes;
        who gives food to all flesh.

(See vv. 4-25.)

The canvas upon which the psalmist here paints the praise of God is indeed enormous. In a few very succinct verses, the psalm paints the greatness of God in his work from creation to his gift of the Promised Land to Israel. In other words, one has here an outline of the first six books of the Bible. And we may be certain that Israel sang about the mighty deeds of her God before she wrote them down as historical narrative.

Psalm 114 represents an example of a hymn that centers on a single or narrow perspective. In this case the emphasis is on the redemption of Israel. God has redeemed Israel by bringing her out of Egypt and into the Promised Land.

A second factor to be noted in the main section of the hymn concerns the way in which God is referred to. The majority of the hymns refer to God in the third person. That is, they praise God not in direct address but in statements and acclamations about God. This is a general characteristic of hymns as opposed to prayers of direct address. Some hymns, however, praise God in direct address, referring to the deity in the second person. The two most notable examples of hymns of direct address are Psalms 8 and 104.

O Lord, our Lord,
    how majestic is thy name in all the earth!
Thou whose glory above the heavens is chanted
    by the mouth of babes and infants,
thou hast founded a bulwark because of thy foes,
    to still the enemy and the avenger.
When I look at thy heavens, the work of thy fingers,
    the moon and the stars which thou hast established;
what is man that thou art mindful of him,
    and the son of man that thou dost care for him?
                                   (Psalm 8:1-4)

O Lord my God, thou art very great!
Thou art clothed with honor and majesty,
    who coverest thyself with light as with a garment,
who hast stretched out the heavens like a tent,
    who hast laid the beams of thy chambers on the waters,
who makest the clouds thy chariot,
    who ridest on the wings of the wind,
who makest the winds thy messengers,
    fire and flame thy ministers.
                                 (Psalm 104:1-4)

How is this major difference in the manner of address in the hymns of praise to be explained? Why was God most frequently praised in the third person but sometimes praised by being addressed directly? Psalm 89 perhaps can offer some help in understanding this phenomenon. This psalm begins with a hymn of praise addressed to the deity (89:1-18). Following this is a section which quotes the content of the promises made by God to the earthly King David (89:19-37). Psalm 89:38-45 describes the treatment and humiliation which the king has undergone at the hand of God. The latter part of the psalm (89:46-51) contains a prayer or petition to God that he would remember the promises made to David and thus no longer leave the king humiliated and forsaken. Psalm 89, therefore, suggests that the hymns in which God was directly addressed were sometimes related to prayers or requests on behalf of the community or individual. In other words, hymns of direct address were often part of the ritual and preparation prior to the making of an appeal to the deity. This use of the hymn as a prelude to an appeal or petition is known from other Near Eastern cultures. The general hymn which spoke of God in the third person would have been used when praise and not petition was the primary focus of the worship service.

In addition to the call to worship (the introit) and the main section (the hymn proper), hymns of praise contained a concluding statement which varied from hymn to hymn. Sometimes this concluding section was a general expression of hope.

> May the Lord give strength to his people!
> May the Lord bless his people with peace!
> (Psalm 29:11)

Frequently, the concluding statement merely repeats the opening words of the psalm. This is the case with Psalms 146–150 which all begin and end with the cry "Hallelujah" or "Praise the Lord." Occasionally the hymns conclude with a call to bless the Lord (Psalm 135:19-21) or with a request (Psalm 104:35) or with a vow (Psalm 115:18). Sometimes the hymns have no distinctive concluding formula or statement.

THE USE OF THE HYMNS OF PRAISE

Just as there are two basic forms of address to God—petition and praise—which are universally found in religion, there are also two basic moods of human sentiment expressed in worship. On the one hand, there is worship oriented to sorrow, mourning, lamenting, contrition, confession, and supplication. This element in religion is concerned with sadness, sin, suffering, and death. In the Christian faith, the season of Lent and especially the worship on Good Friday manifest this mood. On the other hand, there is worship characterized by the experience of joy, triumph, happiness, celebration, jubilation, and thanksgiving. This element in religion celebrates redemption, forgiveness, victory, and the triumph of life over death. In the Christian faith, Easter services manifest this mood of worship.

Hymns of praise, as a rule, give expression to this second mood of worship. They partake of a spirit of celebration and joy. In ancient Israel such psalms were used on those occasions in life and during the course of the year when the community was acutely aware of their experience of divine blessing and concern. The seasonal and festival celebrations were the most obvious occasions in ancient Israel when God was praised. Nonetheless, spontaneous occasions presented themselves when hymns of praise were appropriate.

The celebration of victory in battle was obviously a time when unscheduled praise of God was in order. One of the earliest specimens of an Israelite hymn is found in the celebration of the triumph of God over the Egyptians at the Red Sea. After the crossing of the sea, the prophetess Miriam and all the women are said to have danced to the rhythm of timbrels while Miriam sang a hymn of praise:

> "Sing to the Lord, for he has triumphed gloriously;
> the horse and his rider he has thrown into the sea."
>
> (Exodus 15:21)

After a battle in which the Canaanites were defeated, the prophetess Deborah and the military commander Barak are said to have sung a hymn in praise of God which describes the course of battle and the eventual triumph over the enemy (Judges 5). Such praise of God on the battlefield after victory must have been a common occurrence in early Israel. This was a time when the exuberance and joyful delight of the warriors and their womenfolk burst into song praising God.

These two examples of hymnic praise from the earliest period of Israel's history can be paralleled with examples drawn from Jewish history during the Maccabean struggles a thousand years later. During the Maccabean wars, several references are made to the heroes and their troops praising God "with hymns and thanksgiving" after victory, either on the battlefield itself or else in Jerusalem (1 Maccabees 4:24; 5:54; 13:51; 2 Maccabees 10:7, 38). After the temple was recaptured from the Greeks and rededicated and their fortress destroyed in Jerusalem, these occasions were times for singing hymns of praise (1 Maccabees 13:51; 2 Maccabees 10:7). Throughout Israel's history, the people offered their hymns of praise as they assembled in joyous victory celebrations. One can assume that special hymns were composed and offered for these very specific occasions, but little or none of this material has survived in the book of Psalms (see Psalms 18:31-48; 68:11-23; 118:15-16). Probably during most victory celebrations, the traditional hymns of praise were sung and no special compositions made.

One can imagine other spontaneous occasions in Israel when celebrations praising God would have been appropriate: in the fields as the crops were harvested; in the villages when rain came after drought; in the cities when caravans returned safely. Anytime after some danger or threat had been removed would have provided a proper situation for services of praise and thanksgiving.

Undoubtedly, the major spring and fall festival seasons provided those annual recurring occasions for services of praise. During these periods of festive celebration, enormous throngs went on pilgrimage to the sanctuaries. There they worshiped God offering gifts and sacrifices, enjoying festive meals, rejoicing with music and dance, and recounting the greatness and mercy of the divine in word and hymn. As we noted in the first chapter, these two seasonal celebrations tended to focus upon the great redemption from Egypt, the occupation of the land of Canaan, and the rule of God over history, creation, and his Chosen People. These themes resound through numerous psalms of praise.

HYMNS OF PRAISE AND SPRING CELEBRATIONS

In ancient Israel, the spring of the year was a time of harvest. The cereal crops—barley and wheat—were reaped and brought to the village threshing areas by the farmers. The spring was also the time of newborn animals, when the young lambs and kids romped and played, giving to the farmers and shepherds renewed hope for the life of their flocks. It was the season when the people could and did experience the blessings of God in concrete ways. If, because of the ever-threatening drought or a too severe winter cold, the fields had not produced abundantly and the flocks had suffered, then the people looked forward with dread and fear to famine, hunger, and want. So when the crops produced and the flocks multiplied, it was a season in which to be thankful for the benefits of living in a land "flowing with milk and honey." The spring was also a time for commemorating the birth of national life, reexperiencing the redemption of Israel from the house of Egyptian slavery, and celebrating the freedom of life under God in their own land.

The spring festivals, of which Passover was the most significant, celebrated Israel's redemption from Egypt. We know from Jewish tradition found in the Mishnah that Psalms 113–118 (the so-called Hallel psalms) were sung as part of the Passover celebrations. While the Passover lambs were being slaughtered in the temple, the Levitical choirs sang these psalms. Again, during the night when the Passover meal was eaten, these psalms were sung by the small groups who ate together the commemorative meal which celebrated the hasty flight from Egypt, the beginning of that journey to the Promised Land.

It is easy to see why these psalms were used on that occasion. Psalm 113 praises God for his concern for the oppressed and the unfortunate.

> He raises the poor from the dust,
>   and lifts the needy from the ash heap,
> to make them sit with princes,
>   with the princes of his people.
> He gives the barren woman a home,
>   making her the joyous mother of children. . . .
>
> (Psalm 113:7-9)

In his redemption of Israel from Egypt, God had taken the child of a threatened mother and raised him (Moses) to sit with princes. Although this psalm was probably not originally written about Moses and the Exodus, its selection for singing on the celebration of that occasion was certainly appropriate. It illustrates the Exodus theme—from oppression to freedom, from servitude to service, from humiliation to joy. Or as the Mishnah says about the Passover instruction of the father to the son concerning the story of the Exodus—"He begins with the disgrace and ends with the glory" (Pesahim 10:4).[1]

Psalm 114 is a hymn of praise extolling God for rescuing his people from Egypt. This psalm will be discussed in detail shortly. Psalm 115 is a hymn praising God and comparing him with the idols of the nations. The God of Israel is described as one who in heaven does whatever he pleases, and what he pleases to do is to be mindful of Israel and bless her. He is their help and shield (Psalm 115:9-13). The idols of the nations, their gods, on the other hand, are miserable substitutes for divinity.

> Their idols are silver and gold,
>   the work of men's hands.
> They have mouths, but do not speak;
>   eyes, but do not see.
> They have ears, but do not hear;
>   noses, but do not smell.
> They have hands, but do not feel;
>   feet, but do not walk;
>   and they do not make a sound in their throat.
> Those who make them are like them;
>   so are all who trust in them.
>
> (Psalm 115:4-8)

---

[1] *The Mishnah,* trans. Herbert Danby (London: Oxford University Press, 1933), p. 150. Used by permission of Oxford University Press.

No nation in antiquity knew a greater use of idols than Egypt, who worshiped gods in practically every form. But it was the God of Israel who showed his power and demonstrated the ineffectiveness of the Egyptian gods and idols when he led Israel in the Exodus.

Psalms 116 and 118 are psalms of thanksgiving. (Psalm 117, the shortest of the psalms, is a hymn of praise extolling God for his steadfast love and faithfulness.) These two psalms were appropriate to the Passover celebrations since they reflect the proper attitude and response of the grateful community.

Psalm 114 is clearly a Passover hymn commemorating the Exodus from Egypt and the entry into the Promised Land. The first Passover was observed on the night of the Exodus from Egypt (Exodus 12). When the Hebrews moved into Canaan, they are said to have observed the Passover before eating the produce of the land and setting out to conquer the territory (Joshua 5:10-12). Thus the Passover represents that final taste of the land of bondage and the first taste of the land of freedom. Therefore, the union of the themes of exodus and conquest in Psalm 114 is exactly what one would expect.

Psalm 114 divides easily into four stanzas. The first, verses 1-2, speaks of the Exodus as a departure from a people of strange language, that is, from a people strange, foreign, and different. The goal and purpose of the Exodus were that Israel and Judah should be God's particular heritage, his special sanctuary, his unique people. The Exodus led the Hebrews from a condition of strangeness and into a relationship of intimacy. This intimate relationship between God and his people was given expression in various ways in the Old Testament. Here the imagery is of something holy, set apart, a sanctuary. For the prophets the imagery was frequently that of bride and groom.

> . . . Thus says the Lord,
> I remember the devotion of your youth,
>   your love as a bride,
> how you followed me in the wilderness,
>   in a land not sown.
> Israel was holy to the Lord,
>   the first fruits of his harvest. . . .
>   (Jeremiah 2:2-3)

In the second stanza, verses 3-4, the sea and the River Jordan appear as parallels. The sea parted when the Hebrews left Egypt

(Exodus 14:21-31) and the Jordan rose up in a heap (Joshua 3:14-17) as they crossed into the Promised Land. In making such statements, the ancient Israelites were describing as the work of God not only the escape from Egypt but also the entry into the Promised Land. Both events were affirmed by the Israelites as marvelous occasions— when "the mountains skipped like rams, the hills like lambs." Through the miracle at the sea, imminent death was transmuted and a new life begun; through the miracle at the Jordan, anticipation was turned into realization. Israel saw the possession of the land as such an integral part of her life and faith until she could hardly speak of her entry except in terms of the miraculous. In Egypt and the Promised Land, one must see more than historical realities; they were highly symbolic metaphors—Egypt represented servitude, estrangement, alienation, death and the Promised Land represented freedom, home, brotherhood, and life.

The third stanza, verses 5-6, speaks of the actions noted in verses 3-4 as if they were contemporary, a matter of the present. Perhaps we have reflected here the stress on the contemporaneity of the Passover. Every Passover was a reliving and a participation in the original events. There is no better expression of this idea than a passage from the Mishnah which occurs in a section on the observance of Passover.

> In every generation a man must so regard himself as if he came forth himself out of Egypt, for it is written, *And thou shalt tell thy son in that day saying, It is because of that which the Lord did for me when I came forth out of Egypt* [see Exodus 13:9]. Therefore are we bound to give thanks, to praise, to glorify, to honour, to exalt, to extol, and to bless him who wrought all these wonders for our fathers and for us. He brought us out from bondage to freedom, from sorrow to gladness, and from mourning to a Festival-day, and from darkness to great light, and from servitude to redemption (Pesahim 10:5).[2]

There is no mention of the name of God until the fourth stanza, verses 7-8. Perhaps this was used as a stylistic device to heighten the glorification of the divine. The earth is here called upon to tremble at his presence, for God is the one who gives water from the rock. Probably the reason for selecting the episode of the Israelites getting water from the rock (see Exodus 17:6; Numbers 20:11) was its symbolic significance. In the wilderness, God sustained his people with water in the desert. In placing the action in the present (verse 8),

[2] *Ibid.*, p. 151.

at each Passover, Israel recognized and confessed the continued sustaining providence upon which its life depended.

Numerous hymns of praise were probably employed during the spring festivals. The first day of the Passover-Unleavened Bread celebrations was the special day of Passover. The Passover lamb was slaughtered on the fourteenth day of the month of Nisan and eaten that evening, which was the fifteenth of Nisan, since the "day" began at evening. The fifteenth of Nisan was a day of special convocation when all Israelites assembled for worship. Similarly, the seventh day of the celebration was a time of convocation (see Exodus 12:14-16). Fifty days later, the Feast of Weeks or Pentecost which celebrated the harvest of wheat was held. Although this is not referred to explicitly in the Old Testament, the Feast of Weeks (Pentecost) was celebrated at the time when God gave the law to the people on Mount Sinai. The first and seventh days of Passover-Unleavened Bread and the day of Pentecost would have provided occasions for hymns of praise. Psalms 135; 136; and 147 may be seen as hymns appropriate to these celebrations.

Psalm 135 contains a number of themes which run through the Hallel psalms (Psalms 113–118) which would suggest its association with Passover and Unleavened Bread festivities. These themes are the Exodus from Egypt (135:8-9; 114:1-2), the entrance into the Promised Land (135:10-12; 114:3-4), God's doing what he pleases (135:5-6; 115:3), the futility of idols (135:15-18; 115:4-8), and the blessing of and by the various groups in Israel (135:19-21; 115:12-15).

Psalm 135 opens with a call to the servants of God who stand in the temple precincts (in their convocation) to praise God (vv. 1-4). God is to be praised because he has chosen Israel as his unique possession (see Psalm 114:2). Israel then is the creation and possession of God—his people—and they are the ones who can praise him.

Verses 5-7 offer praise to God who does what he pleases and wills on earth and in heaven, but they note in particular that it is God who controls the weather.

> He it is who makes the clouds rise at the end of the earth,
>   who makes lightnings for the rain
>   and brings forth the wind from his storehouses.
>
>   (Psalm 135:7)

Since the spring festivals were harvest festivals, concern with the weather and praise of God for his control of the weather were natural elements for a hymn of praise.

The Exodus and conquest are praised as the work of God in Psalm 135:8-12. Verse 13, addressed directly to God, suggests that choirs or representatives of the congregation offered up most of the hymns (note the "I" in v. 5) but that on occasion the whole congregation burst out in responsive song. Perhaps verse 14 was a priestly response to the congregation. Idols and idolatry are denounced in Psalm 135:15-18. What are impotent idols before the God of Israel who does what he pleases throughout the cosmos? Israel's God has no competition (Psalm 135:5-6). The hymn closes with a call for the various elements of the congregation to bless the Lord (Psalm 135:19-21): the house of Israel (the laymen), the house of Aaron (the priesthood), the house of Levi (the choral groups), and then those that fear the Lord (everyone). Perhaps verse 21 contains the response which each group offered in rotation and then together in a final hallelujah (praise the Lord!).

Psalm 136 is an antiphonal psalm which surveys the great acts of God from creation to the giving of the Promised Land and culminates in a hymnic confession by the people. The God of creation and history is the God who remembers Israel in her oppression, who rescues her from her foes, and who sustains her life (Psalm 136:23-25). The psalm reveals its antiphonal character in the recurring refrain—"for his steadfast love endures for ever"—which follows each half verse. The psalm was no doubt sung by a choir and a responding congregation. In the body of the hymn, verses 4-25, the refrain is repeated twenty-two times, which equals the number of letters in the Hebrew alphabet. Several psalms are alphabetic compositions; that is, the first verse or stanza begins with the first letter of the alphabet, the second with the second letter, and so on. The alphabetic psalms are Psalms 9–10; 25; 34; 37; 111; 112; 119; and 145. All the psalms in the book of Lamentations are built on this alphabetic scheme. In addition to being an aid to memory, this alphabetic structure probably was also intent on expressing the concept of totality—as we say, from A to Z. Psalm 136 would, therefore, express the comprehensive character of the encompassing steadfast love of God.

HYMNS OF PRAISE AND AUTUMN CELEBRATIONS

As was noted in chapter 1, the central themes in the autumn celebrations in Israel were the kingship of God, his universal rule, his judgment, and the approach of the life-giving rains. A number of the hymns of praise were probably used at this time of the year, especially in conjunction with the Feast of Tabernacles.

Psalm 47 provides an excellent example of a hymn proclaiming God's kingship. The psalm may be subdivided as follows: the call to praise (1-4), the enthronement of God (5-7), and the reign of God (8-9). The call to praise calls upon all peoples to shout to God with songs of joy. Israel's God is here proclaimed as king over the earth who has manifested his kingship in subjecting nations to Israel, whom he has chosen and made the object of his love. This call to praise illustrates the double claim of Israel: God is a universal sovereign but he is in a special and unique way the God of Israel.

The second stanza of the psalm announces that God "has gone up with a shout." How is this to be understood? The answer is probably to be found in the nature and character of the fall festival. The evidence suggests that God annually reentered Jerusalem as king during the celebrations. Psalm 24:7-10 speaks of God entering through the gates as the king of glory. This psalm, which will be discussed in more detail in the next chapter, was used by the worshipers as they entered the sacred precincts. Thus God is portrayed as entering with them. This would suggest that some representation of the deity was carried in procession. Psalm 132 provides the clue as to what was carried. Psalm 132:8 speaks of God arising along with his ark to accompany the people to Zion. Psalm 132 probably doesn't reflect one single event when the ark was brought to Jerusalem but the annual reenactment of the bringing of the ark to Jerusalem. The ark, which was housed in the temple, was probably annually taken from the temple and then carried back to the sanctuary in solemn procession. God again, just as he once had, entered Zion as king. The type of activities associated with God's entrance can be seen in the story of David's bringing the ark to Zion (2 Samuel 6). David brought up the ark amid rejoicing, sacrificing, dancing, shouting, and trumpet blowing (2 Samuel 6:12-15).

> God has gone up with a shout,
>   the Lord with the sound of a trumpet.
> Sing praises to God, sing praises!
>   Sing praises to our King, sing praises!
> For God is the king of all the earth;
>   sing praises with a psalm!
>   (Psalm 47:5-7)

Psalm 47:8-9 speaks of the reign of God who rules over the nations from his holy throne in Zion. The rulers of the peoples are described as gathering to Zion like the people of the God of Abraham (see Isaiah 2:2-4).

Many of the themes characteristic of Psalm 47 reappear in Psalms 93; 95-100. Psalm 93 opens with a proclamation of God's kingship. Like an earthly king, he is described as being dressed in regal robes. The content of the psalm moves from the kingship of God to the theme of creation. The kingship of God is manifest in his establishment of the world. In establishing the world, his throne and divine rule are simultaneously secured (Psalm 93:1-2). This idea of the divine establishment and permanence of the world seems to modern persons a rather insignificant concept. For the ancients it certainly was not, for to them the world was far more uncertain, unknown, and threatening than it is now. In the rhythm of the seasons, people experienced the regularity of nature; but in disease, drought, distress, and death, the ancients experienced life and the world in enigmatic terms. To confess and believe that God had founded the world meant that God's will was seen as the basis of the natural order and that life and the world were under his control and thus possessed an order and rationality. People could live with a certain sense of "at-homeness" in the world and with confidence in the world's operations.

Psalm 93:3-4 proclaims God's rule over chaos and anarchy. He is mightier than the floods, mightier than the thunders of many waters, and mightier than the waves of the sea. The imagery of waters, waves, floods, and the sea has its roots in general Near Eastern thought. In Mesopotamia, where the lands were subject to periodic floods, it was believed that cosmic order and structures ruled over and were created out of turbulent waters. These waters and the depths they represented embodied the constant threat of chaos just as they had at the beginning of creation. In Canaanite religion, the god Baal had to fight and defeat the chaotic waters personified in the god Sea. (Note that it is the sea which God splits to allow the Hebrews to leave Egypt; Exodus 14.) After his defeat of Sea, Baal was acclaimed king of the gods and a house or palace was constructed for him. Much of this Near Eastern imagery has been applied to God in Psalm 93. It is he who establishes the earth and against whom chaotic powers may struggle but over whom they cannot triumph.

The last verse of Psalm 93 is short and terse and has often stumped interpreters. The decrees referred to are probably best understood as the laws established by God to regulate creation. These decrees find reflection in the opening chapter of Genesis, where God is depicted as regulating the orders of creation (see also Genesis 8:22). The idea that God has set bounds and limits to creation occurs in Jeremiah where the prophet compares the regularity and obedience of the "natural world" with the disobedience of Israel.

> . . . I placed the sand as a bound for the sea,
>   a perpetual barrier that it cannot pass;
> though the waves toss, they cannot prevail,
>   though they roar, they cannot pass over it.
> But this people has a stubborn and rebellious heart;
>   they have turned aside and gone away.
> They do not say in their hearts,
>   "Let us fear the Lord our God,
> who gives the rain in its season,
>   the autumn rain and the spring rain,
> and keeps for us
>   the weeks appointed for the harvest."
>
> (Jeremiah 5:22-24)

Elsewhere the prophet compares the permanence of the fixed orders of creation to the eternal character of God's love. (See Jeremiah 31:35-36.)

Just as God created laws to regulate human life and institutions, so also he ordained decrees and laws by which the created order operates. The reference to the house of God in Psalm 93:5 probably does not refer to the earthly temple but instead refers to God's heavenly abode or to the world of creation itself. Just as on earth, cosmic order and holiness befit the house of God. What establishes divine order in the cosmos (Psalm 93:1-2) and subdues the powers of chaos (93:3-4) are God and his decrees (93:5).

A question that arises out of such psalms as 47 and 93 is: were the cosmic orders and the establishment of the world set once and for all by God or were these believed to be annually renewed and reaffirmed in the autumn festival? Psalm 47 pictures God as going up to his throne to assume the kingship. God annually reasserted his role as king. Perhaps the Israelites believed, as did other Near Eastern peoples, that God "re-created" the world, reestablished divine order, and subdued chaos annually in the festival ritual. Parallels to this idea are the Christian concepts of every Christmas as the birth of Christ and every communion service as a reenactment of the death of Jesus.

Psalms 95–99 offer further elaboration of the themes of God as king and of his rulership over creation (Psalms 95:1-4; 96:1-6; 99:1-4). In these psalms, a new emphasis occurs which is not stressed in Psalms 47 and 93. God is depicted as the one who comes in judgment. As we saw in chapter one, the Day of Atonement which was a part of the fall celebrations was, and still is, a day of community judgment and penance in Judaism. Those elements stressing divine judgment in these psalms reflect this aspect of the autumnal festival.

In Psalm 95:8-11, God is pictured speaking directly (through a prophet or priest?) to the community, exhorting them not to be hardhearted and disobedient.

Harden not your hearts, as at Meribah,
  as on the day at Massah in the wilderness
  [see Exodus 17:1-7; Numbers 20:1-13],
when your fathers tested me,
  and put me to the proof, though they had seen my work.
For forty years I loathed that generation
  and said, "They are a people who err in heart,
  and they do not regard my ways."
Therefore I swore in my anger
  that they should not enter my rest.

In this passage, the disobedient generation of the wilderness period is used as the example of what Israel should not be.

The judgment motif is extended in Psalm 96:10-13 to encompass the world of the nations. God is the coming judge who will come to judge the world with righteousness and its people with truth. Psalm 97 describes the judgment and speaks of clouds, thick darkness, fire, and lightnings to illustrate the character of the judgment. The worshipers of idols and all gods are put to shame. Psalm 97:8-9 speaks of the judgments of the adversaries, the idolaters, and the gods as if it were past. "Zion hears and is glad, and the daughters of Judah rejoice, because of thy judgments, O God" (Psalm 97:8). One can imagine that the judgment of God was understood as part of the overall ritual of God's enthronement as king in the temple. In the ritual, there was experienced the triumph of God over all opposition to his rule and will. Psalm 98 describes the judgment as the victory of God but also as an expression of his steadfast love and faithfulness to the house of Israel.

The judgment of God experienced and proclaimed in the worship of the fall festival was, as Psalms 96–98 describe it, a judgment of the nations of the world, the worshipers of images, and other gods (see Psalm 82). Speaking of the judgment on New Year's Day which was part of the autumn celebrations, the Mishnah says: "All that come into the world pass before him like legions of soldiers" (Rosh Ha-Shanah 1:2).[3] It was also a time of special judgment for Israel as well, as can be seen in Psalm 95. Psalm 99 refers to the judgment that fell upon Moses, Aaron, and Samuel (vv. 6-8) and to the fact that God has established equity and executed justice and righteousness in Jacob (v. 4). Thus the days of the festival were times when Israel also was judged and experienced God as an avenger of wrongdoings.

This theme of God's judgment of his people appears in Psalm 81. Verse 3 of this psalm refers to the "feast day" on which the psalm was no doubt used. The heart of this psalm is the address by God in verses 6-16. Reference is made to the redemption from Egypt (Psalm 81:6-7). This is then followed by an exhortation to hear God and to worship him only (Psalm 81:8-10). The following statement in the exhortation reminds one of the opening to the Ten Commandments.

There shall be no strange god among you;
    you shall not bow down to a foreign god.
I am the Lord your God,
    who brought you up out of the land of Egypt. . . .
        (Psalm 81:9-10; compare Exodus 20:1-6)

Early Israel in their stay in the wilderness did not heed and obey the divine voice (Psalm 81:11-12). The contemporary generation is called upon to listen and obey the ways of God (Psalm 81:13) with the promise that blessings would be granted should obedience follow (Psalm 81:14-16).

This stress on the judgment of God upon Israel, the emphasis on the exclusive worship of the Lord, the exhortation to hear and heed the statutes and ways of God, and the promise of blessing all suggest that in the worship of the fall celebrations, the community was presented with the laws of God and challenged to obedience. Exactly when and how this was done in the ritual cannot be precisely reconstructed from the psalms, but Psalm 81 suggests that it was part of a proclamation of judgment upon the past and a call to obedience for the future.

The following passage from the book of Deuteronomy supports

[3] *Ibid.,* p. 188.

the idea that the law was proclaimed with its exhortation to obedience during the fall festivals.

> . . . At the end of every seven years, . . . at the feast of booths, when all Israel comes to appear before the Lord your God at the place which he will choose, you shall read this law before all Israel in their hearing.
>
> (Deuteronomy 31:10-11)

The stipulation of this passage required the reading of the Law, probably the book of Deuteronomy, at the fall festival but only once every seven years. Was there in place of the reading of the full Law the use of some summary of the Law (the Ten Commandments) or such psalms as Psalm 81, which called for absolute obedience during those other years of the seven-year cycle? Evidence suggests that this was the case. Thus in the fall festival, amid celebrations marked by solemn processions, sacred music and dance, sacrifice and song, psalms proclaiming God as king and judge over Israel and the universe, there was the proclamation of the divine will embodied in the Law with a call to a hearing and obedience.

The fall festival marked not only the end of the summer harvest of grapes, fruits, and olives but also the beginning of a new agricultural season. The festival looked forward to the coming year with its promise of blessing and prosperity. In a very concrete way, the life of Palestine was dependent upon the rains which usually began to fall just after the fall festival season. It was only natural that the celebrations of this period would look forward to the coming rains. In late Judaism, there was a special ritual observed during the Feast of Booths which consisted of a water-pouring ceremony. The pouring of water no doubt symbolized and, it was assumed, aided the coming of the "rain in its season."

Psalm 29 may have been employed in the closing worship of the autumn festival cycle. It proclaims and praises God as the Lord of the thunderstorm. The psalm opens with a call to the angelic beings to praise God. There follows a description of the activity of God in terms reflecting the actual path of a Palestinian thunderstorm. The voice or thunder of the Lord upon the waters (vv. 3-4) is reminiscent of the collecting clouds over the Mediterranean. Verses 5-6 depict the storm as it crashes into the Phoenician coast, ripping the cedars and making Mount Hermon (Sirion) dance. The storm moves south toward the desert of Kadesh (vv. 7-8).

> The voice of the Lord makes the oaks to whirl,
>   and strips the forest bare;
>   and in his temple all cry, "Glory!"
>
> (Psalm 29:9)

The psalm concludes with a confession and a benediction. In the storm which brings the life-giving autumn rains that prepare the parched soil for planting, God manifests himself ". . . enthroned over the flood . . . enthroned as king for ever" (Psalm 29:10).

Songs of Zion

3

Jerusalem is a holy city to all three of the world's great monotheistic religions. Judaism reveres the city because it was the site of God's temple, the place where David and his descendants reigned, and the capital city for the ancient Hebrews. The city is sacred to Christians because it was here that Jesus was tried, crucified, and resurrected. For Muslims, Jerusalem is sacred since it was from here that tradition says Muhammad ascended into heaven on his steed Baraq. In Judaism and Christianity, the hopes of the good age to come when God would truly reign on earth were frequently symbolized in the concepts of a new Jerusalem.

Jerusalem, or Zion, is venerated within Judaism to a greater extent than in either Christianity or Islam. Jerusalem as a symbol runs like a sacred, golden thread through the entire fabric of Judaism. As a religion, Judaism has, throughout its history, been closely bound to the concept of a land. This land, in the biblical tradition, was promised to Abraham, was conquered by Joshua and the invading Israelites, was defended and developed by David and his successors, was lost to foreign invaders, was someday to be regained, and was to be transformed at the dawn of the final new age. At the center of the thought of Judaism about the land stood Jerusalem. Since its capture by David, the fortune and fate of the city had been reflective of the fortune and fate of the people. Just as the concept of the land was interwoven into the faith of Judaism, so also was the concept of Zion, the Holy City.

Jerusalem was never understood merely as a secular city or only as a political capital. Jewish historians, prophets, and psalmists understood Zion in theological terms. This theology of Zion was given its clearest expression in the book of Psalms.

PILGRIMAGE TO ZION

Israelite law required that every male should go on pilgrimage three times in the year (Exodus 23:17). These pilgrimages were joyous occasions when groups throughout the land assembled in various villages and set out to Zion. The joys of just the memory of these occasions shine through the following passage:

> These things I remember,
>   as I pour out my soul:
> how I went with the throng,
>   and led them in procession to the house of God,
> with glad shouts and songs of thanksgiving,
>   a multitude keeping festival.
>
> (Psalm 42:4)

When the prophet wished to speak of the delight of the good time coming, he did so in terms of a pilgrimage to the temple: "You shall have a song as in the night when a holy feast is kept; and gladness of heart, as when one sets out to the sound of the flute to go to the mountain of the Lord, to the Rock of Israel" (Isaiah 30:29).

Psalm 84 expresses the yearning desire to visit Jerusalem and stand again in the courts of the temple.

> How lovely is thy dwelling place,
>   O Lord of hosts!
> My soul longs, yea, faints
>   for the courts of the Lord;
> my heart and flesh sing for joy
>   to the living God.
>
> (Psalm 84:1-2)

The psalmist contemplates the advantages which the birds have since they can nest within the temple precincts.

> Even the sparrow finds a home,
>   and the swallow a nest for herself,
>   where she may lay her young,
> at thy altars, O Lord of hosts,
>   my King and my God.
> Blessed are those who dwell in thy house,
>   ever singing thy praise!
>
> (Psalm 84:3-4)

The psalmist cannot live perpetually in the temple, but he can reflect on the joy of the time spent there.

For a day in thy courts is better
    than a thousand elsewhere.
I would rather be a doorkeeper in the house of my God
    than dwell in the tents of wickedness.
                                    (Psalm 84:10)

Psalms 120–134 have as part of their title the expression "A Song of Ascents." This reference probably means that these psalms were used as pilgrim psalms. They were sung as pilgrims prepared for or journeyed on pilgrimage. The spirit of pilgrimage is graphically portrayed in Psalm 122. The psalm opens with a speaker expressing jubilation over pilgrimage.

I was glad when they said to me,
    "Let us go to the house of the Lord!"
                                    (Psalm 122:1)

Then follows perhaps the vocal response of the pilgriming group reflecting the memory of previous visits.

Our feet have been standing
    within your gates, O Jerusalem.
                                    (Psalm 122:2)

The imagery then shifts to a general statement praising Jerusalem and affirming the law of pilgrimage.

Jerusalem, built as a city
    which is bound firmly together,
to which the tribes go up,
    the tribes of the Lord,
as was decreed for Israel,
    to give thanks to the name of the Lord.
                                    (Psalm 122:3-4)

There then follows a plea for prayer on behalf of Jerusalem and a vow to work for her welfare.

Pray for the peace of Jerusalem!
    "May they prosper who love you!
Peace be within your walls,
    and security within your towers!"
For my brethren and companions' sake
    I will say, "Peace be within you!"

> For the sake of the house of the Lord our God,
>   I will seek your good.
>   (Psalm 122:6-9)

ENTRANCE INTO THE SANCTUARY

When pilgrims arrived at the gates of the sacred precincts, entrance rituals played a significant role. Not everyone was allowed inside the temple grounds in antiquity. Persons with physical deformities or persons who were unclean for various reasons were excluded from the arena of the "sacred." Deuteronomy 23:1-8 notes several groups that were not permitted to enter the assembly. It may have been that worshipers wore special garments inside the sacred area (see 2 Kings 10:22). This practice is preserved in such customs as the removal of shoes before entering Muslim mosques, the wearing of special garments within the sacred precincts in Mecca, the use of the skull cap (yarmulke) in Jewish synagogues, and the covering of the head by females in Catholic churches.

The entrance ritual and liturgy for pilgrims to the temple can probably be seen in Psalms 15 and 24. Both of these psalms suggest that worshipers were required to give allegiance to a moral standard of behavior as a condition for entrance.

Psalm 24 opens with a hymnic praise of God.

> The earth is the Lord's and the fulness thereof,
>   the world and those who dwell therein;
> for he has founded it upon the seas,
>   and established it upon the rivers.
>   (Psalm 24:1-2)

This hymn could have been sung by the pilgrims assembled at the gates, by the priests or choirs within the sacred area, or by both groups together.

Both psalms provide us with the inquiries of the pilgrims regarding entrance.

> O Lord, who shall sojourn in thy tent?
>   Who shall dwell on thy holy hill?
>   (Psalm 15:1)

> Who shall ascend the hill of the Lord?
>   And who shall stand in his holy place?
>   (Psalm 24:3)

Response to this inquiry, probably spoken by the priests or gatekeepers, outlines the moral qualities of those to whom admission is granted. Psalm 24 states these in rather general terms.

> He who has clean hands and a pure heart,
>> who does not lift up his soul to what is false,
>> and does not swear deceitfully.
> He will receive blessing from the Lord,
>> and vindication from the God of his salvation.
>>> (Psalm 24:4-5)

Psalm 15 provides a much more elaborate list of qualifications—in fact, ten—which reminds one of the decalogue in Exodus 20 (Deuteronomy 5) and suggests that perhaps the Ten Commandments sometimes may have been used in such entrance liturgies to state the demands of God.

> [1] He who walks blamelessly, and does what is right,
> [2] and speaks truth from his heart;
> [3] who does not slander with his tongue,
> [4] and does no evil to his friend,
> [5] nor takes up a reproach against his neighbor;
> [6] in whose eyes a reprobate is despised,
> [7] but who honors those who fear the Lord;
> [8] who swears to his own hurt and does not change;
> [9] who does not put out his money at interest,
> [10] and does not take a bribe against the innocent.
> He who does these things shall never be moved.
>>> (Psalm 15:2-5)

This list stresses a number of characteristics: uprightness of life, good relationships to friend and neighbor, honor for the faithful and condemnation of the apostate, fidelity to one's word, and an unwillingness to take advantage of the poor or innocent. (Some of the great ethical passages in the prophetical books appear to reflect this practice of proclaiming the demands of God as requirements for entrance to the temple—see Micah 6:6-8; Isaiah 33:15-16; Ezekiel 18:5-9.)

Psalm 15 does not contain the entire entry liturgy. Psalm 24, however, does preserve the remainder of the liturgical responses. The entering pilgrims made confession that they met the requirements for admission.

> Such is the generation of those who seek him,
>> who seek the face of the God of Jacob.
>>> (Psalm 24:6)

Then follows a series of choral/pilgrim responses sung as the gates opened.

> [*Choir/Pilgrims:*] Lift up your heads, O gates!
>   and be lifted up, O ancient doors!
>   that the King of glory may come in.
> [*Choir:*] Who is the King of glory?
> [*Pilgrims:*] The Lord, strong and mighty,
>   the Lord, mighty in battle!
> [*Choir/Pilgrims:*] Lift up your heads, O gates!
>   and be lifted up, O ancient doors!
>   that the King of glory may come in.
> [*Choir:*] Who is this King of glory?
> [*Pilgrims:*] The Lord of hosts,
>   he is the King of glory!
>   (Psalm 24:7-10)

THE ZION PSALMS

Several psalms, among them Psalms 46; 48; 76; 87; and 125, present the theological claims which undergirded ancient Israel's beliefs about Zion. Central to Israel's beliefs about Zion were several concepts. God had chosen Zion as his select dwelling place. He had established his sanctuary there in the form of the temple. In Jerusalem, God reigned as king. The sacred city and its temple enjoyed divine protection.

> . . . he chose the tribe of Judah,
>   Mount Zion, which he loves.
> He built his sanctuary like the high heavens,
>   like the earth, which he has founded for ever.
>   (Psalm 78:68-69; see also Exodus 15:17-18)

Psalm 46, which was the inspiration for Martin Luther's hymn "A Mighty Fortress Is Our God," proclaims the stability and security of Zion in the midst of cosmic chaos and international turmoil. The psalm opens with a confession of confidence in God.

> God is our refuge and strength,
>   a very present help in trouble.
>   (Psalm 46:1)

The world may be threatened by the chaotic waters and the mountains may tremble, but those in Zion have no fear (Psalm 46:2-3). Behind this idea of the threat of chaos and the disarray of creation lies the biblical belief that the world was founded over the waters of chaos. This concept is found in the creation story where God creates order upon the face of the deep and over the face of the waters (Genesis 1:2). In the flood episode, when the world was again returned to its watery state, these foundations of the deep burst forth to inundate the earth (Genesis 7:11). In many Near Eastern cultures, the power of chaos was represented by the sea, sometimes envisioned as a monster to be defeated. Because of God's special protection, Zion had no need even to fear the powers of chaos itself.

Psalm 46:4 speaks of "a river whose streams make glad the city of God, the holy habitation of the Most High." There of course was no actual river that flowed through Zion. The spring Gihon was the city's water source and the brook Kidron only flowed a few weeks in the year during the rainy season. This passage must not be taken literally but must be understood against its background in Near Eastern thought. In this region, the dwelling place of the god or gods was often associated with a mountain from which flowed the streams which watered the earth (see Ezekiel 47:1). This mountain of the god could also be associated with the original paradise (see Ezekiel 28:11-19; Genesis 2:10-14). Zion is here, therefore, identified with the mountain-garden of God. Implicit in this concept is an idea which played an important role in later Judaism: namely, the belief that Jerusalem was the center of the world, the navel of·the universe.

Just as verses 2-3 of this psalm affirm God's protection of Zion against the cosmic threat of chaos, verses 5-6 affirm the stability and security of the city against historical enemies.

> God is in the midst of her, she shall not be moved;
>   God will help her right early.
> The nations rage, the kingdoms totter;
>   he utters his voice, the earth melts.
>   (Psalm 46:5-6)

The worshipers are invited in Psalm 46:8 to come and behold the works of the Lord. God has wrought desolations in the earth and made wars to cease. In other words, God is the source of peace for Zion. One should not think that the psalmist is here referring to any specific battle or victory which God granted his people. One should see this as a cultic celebration in worship of God's rule and the triumph of peace. In like manner, Christians celebrate the salvation of the world through Christ, a reality already experienced but not yet realized.

Psalm 46:10 contains an oracle of God which calls his people to an acceptance of his rule—an acceptance which can be realized in "stillness." This oracle, spoken by some official in worship, a representative of God, expresses the same call as the prophet Isaiah: ". . . In returning and rest you shall be saved; in quietness and in trust shall be your strength . . ." (Isaiah 30:15). God proclaims his rule over the nations and the earth (Psalm 46:10). That is, he rules over the affairs of nations (the historical process) and over the earth (the world of nature). He is a universal ruler but he rules from Zion, his chosen city, at the center of the natural and historical cosmos.

Like Psalm 46, Psalm 48 proclaims the impregnability of Zion—her protection by God from all her enemies. Psalm 48 may be divided into three sections. Verses 1-8 are a hymn in praise of God for his protection of Zion, a hymn which speaks of God in the third person. Verses 9-11 are words of the congregation addressed to God directly, confessing the greatness of God and praising him for his protection of Zion. Verses 12-14 are a call to the worshiping pilgrims to go around Zion so they may proclaim God's greatness to the next generation.

Psalm 48:1-3 describes Zion as God's holy mountain, the joy of all the world, beautiful in elevation. Mount Zion is spoken of as "in the far north." Geographically, however, Zion was not located in the north of Palestine. How then is this statement to be understood? Again, Near Eastern religious concepts provide us with a clue. In the pre-Israelite religion of Canaan, the god Baal was enthroned and ruled as king on Mount Zaphon. The word *zaphon* in Hebrew came to mean "north" because Mount Zaphon was located north of Palestine in Phoenicia. The imagery of the divine ruling on the mount of the north is here applied to God and Zion. Mount Zion is the sacred mountain and it is here that the Lord rules as the divine, great King.

Psalm 48:4-8 speaks of enemy kings who assembled to march against Zion only to be seized by terror and panic and take flight. God acts to protect his city and defend it against its opponents. Again, the reader should not ask about a specific historical event which might lie behind the assault on Zion described in this psalm. What is described here is the confidence which the people had in God's protection of Zion. It is cultic, symbolic imagery which is involved. In the community's celebration and proclamation of the divine protection of the city, the enemies are described as attacking, being astounded, and fleeing; but the enemies are any and all opponents against God and his Holy City. One would certainly not attack Jerusalem, which was miles inland, with ships (see Psalm 48:7). Psalm 48:8—"As we have heard, so have we seen in the city of the Lord of hosts"—might suggest that at one of their festivals the people dramatically acted out the assault against Zion and the flight of the enemies. This could have occurred at the fall festival which celebrated the kingship of God. These same ideas occur in the psalm now found in Exodus 15:1-18, where the enemies are identified as Philistia, Edom, Moab, and the inhabitants of Canaan. Psalm 48, like 46, proclaims and praises God for his divine protection of his city, and this is what the psalm celebrates, not some particular battle or victory.

The prayer addressed to God in Psalm 48:9-11 demonstrates that it was "in the midst of thy temple" that the people gave thought to the love of God expressed in his care for Zion. The people confessed that the true response to such love was praise, rejoicing, and gladness.

A third Zion psalm is Psalm 76, which contains the same structure as Psalm 48. Psalm 76 opens with a hymn in praise of Zion (verses 1-3); contains a hymn addressed to God in verses 4-10; and concludes with an appeal to the participating worshipers. The opening hymn proclaims Zion (=Salem; see the name Jeru*salem*) as the abode and dwelling place of God. The concept of God's dwelling in Zion was based upon the presence of the ark of God in the temple. From several narratives in the Old Testament, we know that the ark was closely associated with the presence of God. Where the ark was, there was God. The ark was considered God's throne (Numbers 10:35-36; 1 Samuel 4:4) and was taken into battle so God could aid the Israelite forces. The ark was box-shaped, carried on poles, and decorated with cherubim, which were probably composite figures with human faces, bull bodies, and bird wings (Exodus 25:10-22). Two huge cherubim with fifteen-foot wing spans stood over the ark in the holy of holies of the Jerusalem temple. When David brought the ark to Jerusalem (2 Samuel 6), it was with great fanfare and all the features of a solemn religious procession. Psalm 132 recalls David's promise to find God a dwelling place.

> Remember, O Lord, in David's favor,
>   all the hardships he endured;
> how he swore to the Lord
>   and vowed to the Mighty One of Jacob, . . .
> "I will not give sleep to my eyes

> or slumber to my eyelids,
> until I find a place for the Lord,
> a dwelling place for the Mighty One of Jacob."
> (Psalm 132:1-5)

When the temple was completed by Solomon, the ark was placed in the sacred holy of holies (1 Kings 8:6). The presence of the ark in the temple meant that God was there; the temple was his dwelling place.

> In Judah God is known,
> his name is great in Israel.
> His abode has been established in Salem,
> his dwelling place in Zion.
> (Psalm 76:1-2)

Psalm 76:3 refers, as did Psalms 46 and 48, to God's triumph and the destruction of the weapons of war. Many interpreters have sought in this verse (and Psalm 76:5-9) a reflection of David's defeat of the Philistines in the environs of Jerusalem (2 Samuel 5:17-25). However, what we have in this passage is cultic terminology. In the worship services God was proclaimed as the king over nations and creation and as victorious over all his and Israel's enemies, historical and otherwise.

The second section of this psalm, verses 4-10, is a hymn praising God. God is here described as terrible in his anger, as one who pronounces judgment upon the earth, and as one who stands in judgment to save the oppressed of the earth. The judgment proclaimed is not judgment against God's own people but judgment upon the enemies of Zion.

The psalm concludes with a call to the worshipers to make their vows and to perform them and to offer gifts to God, who cuts off the rulers of the earth (Psalm 76:11-12). The laws regulating the pilgrim festivals required that "none should appear before [God] empty-handed" (Exodus 23:15). That is, the people must offer to God sacrifices on these occasions. The making of vows—resolutions and promises—at festive celebrations is reflected in the story of Hannah and her husband in 1 Samuel 1. Hannah was childless and prayed that she would become the mother of a child. As part of her request, she vowed to give the child to God if it were a son (1 Samuel 1:11). After the child was born and weaned, Hannah offered him at the sanctuary to fulfill her vow to God. Her husband, Elkanah, was said to have gone up to Shiloh every year to offer sacrifice and to pay his vow (1

Samuel 1:21). This yearly festival attended by Elkanah was no doubt the great autumn festival, a time when people made commitments to God, binding vows for the coming year.

At this point, perhaps we should summarize the Israelite beliefs about Zion as these found expression in the psalms and were celebrated in worship. (1) God had chosen Zion out of all the cities as his special place. (2) Zion was the dwelling place of God and the sanctuary his abode. (3) Zion was identified with the cosmic divine mountain from which flowed the life-giving streams. (4) God was the protector of Zion, defending her against the threat of chaotic waters and the onslaught of national and historical enemies. (5) In Zion, God was the great King ruling over his people, the nations, and cosmic order.

The blessings and benefits that came to Zion and her people were the gifts of God.

> For the Lord has chosen Zion;
>   he has desired it for his habitation.
> "This is my resting place for ever;
>   here I will dwell, for I have desired it.
> I will abundantly bless her provisions;
>   I will satisfy her poor with bread.
> Her priests I will clothe with salvation,
>   and her saints will shout for joy.
> There I will make a horn to sprout for David;
>   I have prepared a lamp for my anointed.
> His enemies I will clothe with shame,
>   but upon himself his crown will shed its luster."
>   (Psalm 132:13-18)

The city of Zion and the family of David were closely associated in Israelite theology, as the last four lines of the above passage illustrate. The psalms concerned with the house of David will be discussed in chapter 6.

The significance of being a citizen of Zion is the subject of Psalm 87. Interpreters are uncertain about how to understand Psalm 87:4. Does it refer to Israelites who live in the countries referred to? Or does it signify that these states recognize the God of Israel? At any rate, Psalm 87:5-6 seems clear enough. To have been born in Zion carries a special citizenship. As God registers the people of the world, he will make special reference to those having been born in Zion. The register referred to here denotes the heavenly books on which it was assumed God keeps records. This idea of heavenly registers or books was a rather widespread concept in the ancient world. Sometimes the reference is to a heavenly book on which a person's entire life was written (Psalm 139:16), or the woes and judgments to fall upon a people (Ezekiel 2:8-10), or the deeds for which judgment was to be handed down (Daniel 7:10). The Babylonians believed that the gods met once a year, in conjunction with the New Year celebrations, to determine and write down the fate of the people for the coming year. Our practice of determining a new fate for ourselves with New Year's resolutions has a long history! The divine registration of the peoples referred to in Psalm 87:6 suggests the belief that God preserves a record of humankind, but that being a citizen of Zion is noted as conferring a special status.

The divine protection and care for Zion could be used in Jewish thought as a pattern for the Lord's care for those who trusted in him.

> Those who trust in the Lord are like Mount Zion,
>   which cannot be moved, but abides for ever.
> As the mountains are round about Jerusalem,
>   so the Lord is round about his people,
>   from this time forth and for evermore.
>   (Psalm 125:2)

ZION OUTSIDE THE PSALMS

The Israelite belief in God's special care and protection of Zion was fraught with the possibility of being understood in an artificial and overconfident fashion. The Zion theology could be understood as a promise of God's automatic protection of the city regardless of the attitude and fidelity of the people. Several of the prophets attacked the beliefs associated with Zion and proclaimed the coming judgment upon the city.

The prophet Micah, about 725 B.C., denounced the Israelite people and the citizens of Zion for their wickedness and perversion of justice and proclaimed the judgment of God, which would result in the destruction of Jerusalem.

> Hear this, you heads of the house of Jacob
>   and rulers of the house of Israel,
> who abhor justice
>   and pervert all equity,
> who build Zion with blood
>   and Jerusalem with wrong.

> Its heads give judgment for a bribe,
>   its priests teach for hire,
>   its prophets divine for money;
> yet they lean upon the Lord and say,
>   "Is not the Lord in the midst of us?
>   No evil shall come upon us."
> Therefore because of you
>   Zion shall be plowed as a field;
> Jerusalem shall become a heap of ruins,
>   and the mountain of the house a wooded height.
>   (Micah 3:9-12)

Micah condemns the false security associated with Zion in which the people claimed an immunity from judgment and disaster because of God's presence in Jerusalem. Zion, the prophet declared, cannot expect divine protection when the rulers, priests, and prophets were unconcerned for justice and equity but were primarily desirous of economic gain.

Isaiah, a prophetic contemporary of Micah, denounced Jerusalem in very similar terms.

> How the faithful city
>   has become a harlot,
>   she that was full of justice!
> Righteousness lodged in her,
>   but now murderers.
> Your silver has become dross,
>   your wine mixed with water.
> Your princes are rebels
>   and companions of thieves.
> Every one loves a bribe
>   and runs after gifts.
> They do not defend the fatherless,
>   and the widow's cause does not come to them.
>   (Isaiah 1:21-23)

The sharpest dialogue with the Zion theology was offered by the prophet Jeremiah. The Book of Jeremiah preserves two parallel versions of the prophet's attack on the false security associated with Zion (see Jeremiah 7 and 26). According to this account, the prophet took a position in the gates or the court of the temple in order to denounce the people. His selection of the temple as the place of his preaching was no doubt related to the fact that the Zion theology was proclaimed in the psalms used in worship. Perhaps it was also the time of one of the major festivals, a time when these psalms would have been used and when throngs of pilgrims would have made their way to the city of God (Psalm 87:3).

Jeremiah preached that the worshipers should not place their faith in the security of Zion and the belief that God would defend his dwelling place. "Do not trust in these deceptive words: 'This is the temple of the Lord, the temple of the Lord, the temple of the Lord'" (Jeremiah 7:4). Jeremiah demanded, in the name of God, that the people amend their ways and change their behavior. Otherwise God would destroy the temple just as he had destroyed Shiloh, one of the earliest shrines of Israel (Jeremiah 7:5-15).

For his caustic diatribe against the people and the temple, Jeremiah was placed under arrest and put on trial. The priests and the prophets, that is, the religious establishment, demanded death— "This man deserves the sentence of death, because he has prophesied against this city" (26:11). Jeremiah was saved from death through the aid of some princes and other people. Significant in his case was the precedent of Micah's prediction concerning the destruction of Jerusalem (26:16-19). Since Micah had received no punishment, it was argued, neither should Jeremiah.

This conflict between Jeremiah and the worshipers in Jerusalem demonstrates how significant the Zion theology was. God's special relationship to and defense of Zion were tenets of Israel's faith which could be challenged only at the risk of being considered a traitor.

In addition to the prophet's head-on attack against the overconfident trust in the invulnerability of Zion, they also challenged the Zion claims by projecting the significant role of Zion into the future. The claims made for Zion by the prophets were not related to the present—which they saw as a time of infidelity—but were proclaimed as a utopian condition to be realized in the future. Thus by proclaiming the role of the Zion of the future, the prophets were indirectly placing the present under judgment. Not the Zion of the present but the Zion of the future will be the realization of God's will. Isaiah 2:2-4 and Micah 4:1-4 contain almost identical passages concerning the significance and role of the future Zion. Whether one prophet was dependent upon the other, or both were dependent upon traditional Zion material or these passages were added to the books at a time later than the prophets can no longer be determined. At any rate, the passages clearly speak of the future importance of Zion.

It shall come to pass in the latter days
  that the mountain of the house of the Lord
shall be established as the highest of the mountains,
  and shall be raised up above the hills;
and peoples shall flow to it,
  and many nations shall come, and say:
"Come, let us go up to the mountain of the Lord,
  to the house of the God of Jacob;
that he may teach us his ways
  and we may walk in his paths."
For out of Zion shall go forth the law,
  and the word of the Lord from Jerusalem.
He shall judge between many peoples,
  and shall decide for strong nations afar off;
and they shall beat their swords into plowshares,
  and their spears into pruning hooks;
nation shall not lift up sword against nation,
  neither shall they learn war any more;
but they shall sit every man under his vine and under his fig tree,
  and none shall make them afraid;
  for the mouth of the Lord of hosts has spoken.

                                          (Micah 4:1-4)

Several factors in this passage are noteworthy. (1) It concerns and projects what is expected to take place in some indeterminate future (in the latter days) when Zion will fulfill her true role. (2) The temple mount will be elevated to be the highest of mountains; that is, it will be the point of unity between the earthly and the heavenly worlds. (3) The nations of the earth shall come in pilgrimage to Zion just as previously the Israelite tribes had journeyed to Jerusalem. Zion will become the true center of the world. (4) The law of God will be taught from Zion and will be learned by the nations. (5) God will function as the judge and arbitrator in international disputes. (6) International strife and warfare will cease as a result, and the instruments of battle shall be transformed into tools for human betterment. (7) Everyone will be able to live in peace, content with self and surroundings, and unafraid.

When Zion fell to the onslaught of the Babylonian forces in 586 B.C., this was the most traumatic event in Jewish history. The city was burned and its fortifications pulled down. The temple was looted and burned. The rule of the Davidic family came to an end. Jewish independence and national self-determination were lost. It was a challenge to the whole of Jewish life and faith, but especially to the claims and promises associated with Zion.

The people taken into exile were chided by their captors to sing the songs of Zion, chided to sing those old psalms of Zion which proclaimed the greatness of the city and its divine protection. The exiles could not sing Zion's song in a foreign land, but neither could they forget Jerusalem (see Psalm 137).

The agony and the sadness of the fall of Jerusalem are given graphic expression in the five poems found in the book of Lamentations. These are psalms of distress, composed and sung, one might say, amid the ruins and ashes of a desolate Zion. These poems were used in services of public fasting and mourning which were held on the ninth day of the month of Ab (late summer), a day which commemorated the disaster. The desolation of Zion is reflected in practically every passage in the book. The great festivals which celebrated the grandeur of Zion and her God were no longer held. No longer did throngs pilgrimage to the city to fill its precincts with joy, music, and dance (see Lamentations 1:4). The destruction of Jerusalem was not attributed, however, to either the caprice of history or to the superior strength of the Babylonians. It was the work of God against his own people and his own city (see Lamentations 2:1, 5-6).

The actions of God are not attributed to unmotivated whim. The laments point to the sins of Zion as the reason for her troubles. It was the sin of Jerusalem (Lamentations 1:8) which led to her destruction, for in annihilating Zion "the Lord has done what he purposed, has carried out his threat; as he ordained long ago . . ." (Lamentations 2:17).

Even the book of Lamentations is not without hope, for it entreats God to view the plight of his people and take action on behalf of Zion (see Lamentations 3:19-23).

The Zion theology was not smothered in the ashes of Jerusalem. It was transposed to a new key. The prophets, after the destruction of the city, spoke of the new glory of Zion to come (see Isaiah 40:1; 49:14-26; Jeremiah 30:12-22). The Zion psalms with their marvelous claims and promises were not discarded but were no doubt sung in anticipation of the new, the true, the ideal Zion to come. When the Christian prophet authored the book of Revelation, he could choose no better picture with which to portray the ideal age to come than the new Jerusalem (Revelation 21).

4

Personal Psalms
of Distress

The misery of life's misfortunes, the desperation of human distress, the anguish of personal adversity, and the agony of mortal affliction came to expression in ancient Israel's psalms of personal calamity. These psalms appeal to God for divine help out of situations characterized by individual tribulation, or as Psalm 130:1 says: "Out of the depths I cry to thee, O Lord."

Psalms of distress or laments in which the individual gives expression to difficulties and petitions God for assistance comprise the largest group within the Psalter. Over fifty psalms belong to this type. Such a number denotes that ancient Israel could be compassionately concerned about the individual who experienced suffering and offered supplication.

Laments belong to the crisis situations of life. They are the products of the crucible of distress. In the ordinary course of life, people encounter conditions which threaten their well-being, even their very existence, and which challenge their faith and trust. The worship of ancient Israel sought to deal with such situations and to offer the worshipers means for contact with the divine. Such means were prayer and sacrifice. When sickness and disease, personal calamity, sin, and adversity struck, the Old Testament worshiper could present the situation to God and, in psalm and sacrifice, could appeal to the divine. The laments of the psalms were no doubt elements in a complex of ritual. One should, in a fashion, read the book of Leviticus, with its rituals for sacrifice, and the book of Psalms, with its prayers, in parallel columns. Psalm and sacrifice, ritual and spoken word go together.

The laments which we find in the Psalter, as well as the other psalms, were no doubt used on many occasions. They were not written for one special time of use. In fact, we should probably assume that many were officially written and then offered by worshipers as the need presented itself. To this extent, the laments tend to employ stereotyped language and formulas, just as prayers always have. Thus the "I" that speaks may have been many individuals on different occasions throughout Israel's history. Indeed, many of the very personal psalms could have been employed by the whole congregation or by groups who saw themselves in the "I" that addresses God.

THE STRUCTURE OF THE LAMENT

In the lament or psalm of distress, the individual presented his condition and case before the deity and pleaded for divine action on his behalf. Practically all of the laments follow a common pattern since they reflect the address of a troubled man to his God. The following elements occur in the outline of the lament, although in some psalms individual items may be missing or greatly elaborated.

1. *Address to God.* The lament opens with a direct address to God and may contain a brief statement of appeal or a short confession of confidence.
2. *Description of Distress.* This section depicts the conditions under which the person is living and from which he wishes to be saved. Sometimes, the description of the distress is expressed in terms of a complaint against God.
3. *Plea for Redemption.* This element enunciates the worshiper's request to God; it is his appeal for help. Frequently, this plea takes a double form. The one praying asks that he be saved from his crisis and that his enemies be punished or annihilated. The plea then often contains both a positive and a negative appeal.
4. *Statement of Confidence.* Here the worshiper expresses his confidence in God and his assurance of a favorable hearing. Most frequently this is spoken directly to God in the form of first-person address, although the statement of confidence sometimes speaks of God in the third person, which would suggest that the confession was addressed to some human audience—to the priests or other worshipers present.
5. *Confession of Sin or Affirmation of Innocence.* Sometimes, the one praying confesses that sin is the cause of his calamity. At other times, the worshiper, like Job, refuses to see his adversity as a result of his wrongdoing.

6. *Pledge or Vow.* In this section, the worshiper promises to perform certain acts if his prayer is heard.

7. *Conclusion.* This may consist of hymnic praise of the deity, a restatement of the plea, a blessing, and so on.

Specific examples of these components of the lament will illustrate the character, form, and content of the lament.

1. *Address to God:*

> Answer me when I call, O God of my right!
> (Psalm 4:1)
> Give ear to my words, O Lord;
> give heed to my groaning.
> (Psalm 5:1)
> O Lord, rebuke me not in thy anger,
> nor chasten me in thy wrath.
> (Psalm 6:1)
> Out of the depths I cry to thee, O Lord.
> (Psalm 130:1)

2. *Description of Distress:*

> Be gracious to me, O Lord, for I am in distress;
> my eye is wasted from grief,
> my soul and my body also.
> For my life is spent with sorrow,
> and my years with sighing;
> my strength fails because of my misery,
> and my bones waste away.
> (Psalm 31:9-10)

An example of the distress formulated as a complaint against God is the following:

> How long, O Lord? Wilt thou forget me for ever?
> How long wilt thou hide thy face from me?
> How long must I bear pain in my soul,
> and have sorrow in my heart all the day?
> How long shall my enemy be exalted over me?
> (Psalm 13:1-2)

3. *Plea for Redemption:* The plea for deliverance was the worshiper's request for a divine hearing and response.

> I call upon thee, for thou wilt answer me, O God;
> incline thy ear to me, hear my words.

> Wondrously show thy steadfast love,
>> O savior of those who seek refuge
>> from their adversaries at thy right hand.
> Keep me as the apple of the eye;
>> hide me in the shadow of thy wings,
> from the wicked who despoil me,
>> my deadly enemies who surround me.
>> (Psalm 17:6-9)

When the worshiper saw himself plagued by enemies, his plea to the divine requested that his enemies be opposed or destroyed.

> Arise, O Lord! confront them, overthrow them!
>> Deliver my life from the wicked by thy sword,
> from men by thy hand, O Lord,
>> from men whose portion in life is of the world.
> May their belly be filled with what
>> thou hast stored up for them;
>> may their children have more than enough;
>> may they leave something over to their babes.
>> (Psalm 17:13-14)

4. *Statement of Confidence:* Most frequently this is addressed directly to God.

> Yea, thou art my rock and my fortress;
>> for thy name's sake lead me and guide me,
> take me out of the net which is hidden for me,
>> for thou art my refuge.
> Into thy hand I commit my spirit;
>> thou hast redeemed me, O Lord, faithful God.
>> (Psalm 31:3-5)

Some of the assertions of confidence seem to have been addressed to other worshipers in attendance rather than directly to God.

> I cry aloud to the Lord,
>> and he answers me from his holy hill.
> I lie down and sleep;
>> I wake again, for the Lord sustains me.
> I am not afraid of ten thousands of people
>> who have set themselves against me round about.
>> (Psalm 3:4-6)

5. *Confession of Sin or Affirmation of Innocence:* In some of the laments, a direct relationship is drawn between the sins of the worshiper and his present calamitous situation.

> For thy name's-sake, O Lord,
> > pardon my guilt, for it is great.
> Turn thou to me, and be gracious to me;
> > for I am lonely and afflicted.
> Relieve the troubles of my heart,
> > and bring me out of my distresses.
> Consider my affliction and my trouble,
> > and forgive all my sins.
> > > (Psalm 25:11, 16-18)

At other times, the one praying denies any guilt and protests his innocence.

> If thou triest my heart, if thou visitest me by night,
> > if thou testest me, thou wilt find no wickedness in me;
> > my mouth does not transgress.
> With regard to the works of men, by the word of thy lips
> > I have avoided the ways of the violent.
> My steps have held fast to thy paths,
> > my feet have not slipped.   (Psalm 17:3-5)

6. *Pledge or Vow:* As his response to the expected answer to his prayer, the worshiper vowed to offer praise and sacrifice to God in thanksgiving. Sometimes this vow is addressed directly to God; at other times it seems to have been addressed to the worshiping audience or the priests.

> Then my tongue shall tell of thy righteousness
> > and of thy praise all the day long.
> > > (Psalm 35:28)

> I will tell of thy name to my brethren;
> > in the midst of the congregation I will praise thee.
> > > (Psalm 22:22)

> My vows to thee I must perform, O God;
> > I will render thank offerings to thee.
> > > (Psalm 56:12)

> I will give to the Lord the thanks due to his righteousness,
> > and I will sing praise to the name of the Lord, the Most High.
> > > (Psalm 7:17)

7. *Conclusion:* The conclusions to the psalms of lament are diverse and reflect no typical pattern. Frequently they end with the statement of a vow or confidence.

> Deliverance belongs to the Lord;
>   thy blessing be upon thy people!
>   (Psalm 3:8)
> For thou dost bless the righteous, O Lord;
>   thou dost cover him with favor as with a shield.
>   (Psalm 5:12)

A number of the laments are characterized by a shift from lament to praise, from anguish to celebration, from mourning to joy. One of the clearest examples of this shift within a lament is Psalm 6. The first seven verses of this psalm lament the condition of the worshiper, describe his distress, and appeal to God for help. Suddenly, the tone of the psalm shifts to a note of assurance and certainty. Psalm 6:8-10 no longer lament; these verses bombastically scold the workers of iniquity and display an assured arrogance. This change in temperament had led many biblical scholars to suppose that two psalms have been combined or to assume that midway in his prayer, the worshiper experienced a deep psychological change. The clue to understanding this shift can be seen in the last half of verse 8 and in verse 9.

> . . . the Lord has heard the sound of my weeping.
> The Lord has heard my supplication;
>   the Lord accepts my prayer.

Here the psalmist claims that God has heard his appeal and granted him a favorable response. How did the worshiper know this? How did he come to realize that God had granted him his request?

Two passages outside the psalms suggest an answer to this question. In 1 Samuel 1, there is the story of Hannah, who was unable to conceive. During the festival at the sanctuary, Hannah went into the temple and, weeping, prayed that God would look on her calamity. She vowed that if she were relieved of the distress of her barrenness she would give the child, if a son, to God. This passage reflects a situation of lament—the barrenness—out of which Hannah wept and lamented and vowed a pledge to God. Here, in other words, one can see the components of the situation of distress and the attempt to resolve it in worship. The old priest at Shiloh, Eli, sees her praying silently but assumes that she has simply been overdrinking in the festivities. When she explains the situation, the priest dismisses her with the assurance that God will grant her the petition.

Hosea 14:1-7 is a second passage which offers some aid in understanding the answered lament. This text contains a call to repentance and prayer to God (14:1-2*a*). The prophet even supplies the confessional prayer (14:2*b*-3). Then follows a response to the prayer spoken by the deity in the first person (14:4-7). This response represents the divine answer to the plea and to the people's vow never again to follow idolatry.

First Samuel 1 and Hosea 14 suggest that divine responses could be offered to the worshiper which granted the one praying an assurance of divine hearing and response. These responses were probably spoken by the cultic officials in the services. There are four psalms which contain divine oracles spoken within the context of a lament for help (Psalms 12:5; 60:6-8; 91:14-16; and 108:7-9). All of these divine responses appear in laments of the community rather than in personal psalms of distress. However, we should probably assume that similar responses were on occasion addressed in the name of the deity to individual worshipers.

Several psalms appear to contain words spoken by the priest to the worshiper, offering encouragement and direction. These occur within lament psalms:

> Offer right sacrifices,
>   and put your trust in the Lord.
>   (Psalm 4:5)

> Wait for the Lord;
>   be strong, and let your heart take courage;
>   yea, wait for the Lord.
>   (Psalm 27:14)

> Love the Lord, all you his saints!
>   The Lord preserves the faithful,
>   but abundantly requites him who acts haughtily.
> Be strong, and let your heart take courage,
>   all you who wait for the Lord!
>   (Psalm 31:23-24)

> Cast your burden on the Lord,
>   and he will sustain you;
> he will never permit
>   the righteous to be moved.
>   (Psalm 55:22)

This type of priestly instruction and admonition to the worshipers may have been very important to the one praying insofar as his faith and assurance were concerned. The whole of Psalm 37 reflects this tone of priestly instruction and assurance to the worshipers.

The lamenting individual probably not only received assurance and response from the cultic officials but also simply from the act of offering prayer and sacrifice in faith. Psalm 5:3 suggests that in prayer and sacrifice the worshiper waited for some response from the deity.

O Lord, in the morning thou dost hear my voice;
in the morning I prepare a sacrifice for thee, and watch.

The reference to the sacrifice in the morning could suggest that a worshiper may have spent the night in the sacred precincts, a common practice throughout the ancient Near East. While sleeping in the temple, the worshiper hoped to find peace with God and receive some divine word. Samuel was spoken to by night (1 Samuel 3); and it was in a dream in the sanctuary at Gibeon that Solomon was promised special divine wisdom (1 Kings 3:3-15). Psalm 4:8 has the psalmist say, "In peace I will both lie down and sleep; for thou alone, O Lord, makest me dwell in safety," but no direct reference is made to a nocturnal sojourn in the temple (see also Psalm 3:4-6).

The combination of lament and jubilation or the two modes of addressing God—petition and praise—within the same psalm should be explained as the result of the worshiper having received a favorable response to his request during the service of lament. The assurance could have come through a consoling word of acceptance, spoken by the priest in his own words, or as an oracle from God. Or the assurance may have been the result of the general act of offering psalm and sacrifice, in which the worshiper himself came to experience the response of God.

LAMENTS OF THE SICK

As we noted in chapter 1, times of illness could be occasions when individuals sought divine help in worship. The form which rituals involving sickness took is discussed in the Old Testament only with regard to certain contagious diseases (Leviticus 13–15). Even in this material, the concern focuses on the priestly determination of the illness' uncleanness and the rituals for reintegrating the unclean into the total life of the community. Thus we are uncertain about the rituals employed when an ordinary ill or diseased person presented appeals to the deity.

In the book of Ecclesiasticus, written about 180 B.C., a Jewish sage described the course which a man should follow when sick. The steps he recommended were prayer, repentance, offering sacrifice, and consulting the physician.

> My son, when you are sick do not be negligent,
>   but pray to the Lord, and he will heal you.
> Give up your faults and direct your hands aright,
>   and cleanse your heart from all sin.
> Offer a sweet-smelling sacrifice,
>   and a memorial portion of fine flour,
>   and pour oil on your offering,
>   as much as you can afford.
> And give the physician his place,
>   for the Lord created him;
>   let him not leave you, for there is need of him.
>   (Ecclesiasticus 38:9-12)

We should therefore think of laments to God as prayers used in conjunction with sacrificial rituals during times of illness.

A number of laments describe the distress of the worshiper in terms of illness and sickness. Among these are Psalms 6, 13, 31, 38, 39, 88, and 102. In Psalm 6, the psalmist describes the misery of his present condition.

> I am weary with my moaning;
>   every night I flood my bed with tears;
>   I drench my couch with my weeping.
> My eye wastes away because of grief,
>   it grows weak because of all my foes.
>   (Psalm 6:6-7)

Elsewhere in the psalm, he speaks of the deterioration of his life—"I am languishing," "my bones are troubled," and "my soul also is sorely troubled." In the plea begging for deliverance, death is spoken of as a place where there is no remembrance of God and Sheol, the realm of the dead, as a place where there is no praise of God. This psalm reflects the stage in Israel's religious pilgrimage prior to the development of a doctrine of meaningful life after death or a concept of resurrection. Death and the dead were an arena separated from God; so the psalmist argues indirectly in his request that God should save him from his condition so that he might continue to praise him.

Psalm 6 seems to attribute the worshiper's illness and distress to "foes" and "workers of evil" (vv. 7-8). These are not attributed to God nor related to any wrongdoing on the part of the individual. Who were these causes of calamity? Were they considered to be demons? We know that in later Judaism, in New Testament times, demons were considered the primary causes of illnesses, especially mental ones. Or were these "workers of evil" the man's enemies or sorcerers hired by his enemies whom he believed had cast spells upon him? The Second Commandment, prohibiting the use of God's name in vain, may have originally been a prohibition against use of the divine name in casting curses or spells upon people. (One should note that most modern profanity is in a way a "prayer"!) The Book of Ezekiel speaks of Israelite women who were hired to use magic in destroying people (Ezekiel 13:17-23).

Like Psalm 6, Psalm 13 speaks of foes and the enemies who are waiting to rejoice over the worshiper's death. The psalmist prays that God will hear his prayer and appeal and answer him before he sleeps the sleep of death.

In many respects, Psalm 31 reminds the reader of the Book of Job. It is permeated with the metaphors and expressions of sickness, but whether one has here an actual usage or merely a poetic one cannot be determined. In the opening stanza (vv. 1-2), the psalm addresses the divine with a plea that God would be a refuge and a fortress. Then follows, in verses 3-8, a long statement of confidence and trust in God, with an affirmation of the psalmist's innocence (v. 6). Following this is the extended description of the worshiper's distress which reminds one of Job's plight.

> Be gracious to me, O Lord, for I am in distress;
>   my eye is wasted from grief,
>   my soul and my body also.
> For my life is spent with sorrow,
>   and my years with sighing;
> my strength fails because of my misery,
>   and my bones waste away.
> I am the scorn of my adversaries,
>   a horror to my neighbors,
> an object of dread to my acquaintances;
>   those who see me in the street flee from me.
> I have passed out of mind like one who is dead;
>   I have become like a broken vessel.
> Yea, I hear the whispering of many—

terror on every side! —
as they scheme together against me,
as they plot to take my life.
(Psalm 31:9-13)

This ostracism, loneliness, and rejection by old friends with its subsequent sorrow and heartache find their parallel in one of Job's laments (Job 19:13-22). Both this passage and Job 19 recall the plight of the leper who during the time of his uncleanness was forced "to wear torn clothes and let the hair of his head hang loose . . . and cry 'Unclean, unclean' . . . [and] dwell alone" (Leviticus 13:45-46). But like Job (Job 19:23-29), the psalmist possessed hope in spite of his misery and proclaimed already the manifestation of God's love toward him (Psalm 31:19-22).

One of the fullest descriptions of the wretchedness of physical suffering is found in Psalm 38. Except for the introductory address (vv. 1-2), a short statement of confidence (v. 15), and a brief plea for help (vv. 21-22), the entire psalm is a description of the worshiper's distress. The calamitous condition of the psalmist is presented in a cacophony of complaints: "no soundness in my flesh . . . no health in my bones . . . My wounds grow foul and fester . . . my loins are filled with burning. . . . My heart throbs, my strength fails me . . . the light of my eyes . . . has gone from me . . . my pain is ever with me." Throughout the psalm, however, the suffering is understood both as divinely sent and as the recompense for sin.

There is no soundness in my flesh
because of thy indignation;
there is no health in my bones
because of my sin.
(Psalm 38:3)

The person attributes his troubles to God's divine wrath: "thy arrows have sunk into me, and thy hand has come down on me" (v. 2). The psalmist recognizes that the judgment under which he mourns is the result of his foolishness, his iniquities, and his sin. This psalm thus clearly draws a connection between human sin, divine indignation, and physical suffering. This view was widely held, although not universally, in ancient Israel. Such a belief could help explain why his friends, companions, and family stood aloof from his suffering and why others sought his life (vv. 11-12, 19-20) even though he was now repentant. If people believed that one received in life what one deserved from God, then to attempt to alleviate an individual's suffering was to interfere in the divine execution of judgment, to frustrate divine purpose.

Like Psalm 38, Psalm 39 relates human suffering and sin to divine chastisement. Three requests are contained in this lament. There is, first of all, the prayer that God would grant the one praying some knowledge of the time of his end. When will this fleeting shadow, this mere breath, of life be over? Second, the prayer requests the deliverance from sin which has brought about the divine chastisement. The man has experienced what he considers the devastating wrath of God.

> When thou dost chasten man
>   with rebukes for sin,
> thou dost consume like a moth what is dear to him.
>
> (Psalm 39:11)

Third, the lament pleads for God to withdraw his gaze and grant the worshiper a moment's respite before the end of his existence.

> For I am thy passing quest,
>   a sojourner, like all my fathers.
> Look away from me, that I may know gladness,
>   before I depart and be no more!
>
> (Psalm 39:12b-13)

One of the most forlorn and despairing laments of the sick is Psalm 88. The psalm speaks of appeals and prayer to the deity day and night (vv. 1-2). In the description of the plight (vv. 3-9, 15-18), the lament depicts the sufferer at the point of death, a condition he seems to have endured from his youth (v. 15). His life is near to Sheol and he counts himself as already reckoned for the Pit. Sheol, the realm of the dead, and the Pit, the collection place for bones in the family sepulchre, are not understood in the Old Testament as places of punishment. They are the abode of the deceased. The one praying sees this realm as a place where the dead are separated forever from the divine: "those whom thou dost remember no more, for they are cut off from thy hand" (v. 5). If death confronts the man with no hope, then so does life. He sees himself as the object of divine wrath and it is God who has brought him to the Pit's door (vv. 6-7). It is God's terrors he endures and whose dreaded assaults are overwhelming him (vv. 15-18). It is God who has made his life a nightmare of forsakenness.

Thou hast caused my companions to shun me;
    thou hast made me a thing of horror to them.
I am shut in so that I cannot escape;
    my eye grows dim through sorrow.

Thou hast caused lover and friend to shun me;
    my companions are in darkness.
                       (Psalm 88:8-9*a*, 18)

The psalmist has reached a stage where he can only hurl his complaints at the deity whom he has known only in misery.

There is practically no glimmer of hope in the lament. He can ask that his prayer be heard (vv. 2, 13), but he displays no confidence— and yet he continues to pray day and night. He brings to God no special appeal, only questions which perhaps he thinks might elicit a divine hearing and divine action before death claims him.

Dost thou work wonders for the dead?
    Do the shades rise up to praise thee?
Is thy steadfast love declared in the grave,
    or thy faithfulness in Abaddon?
Are thy wonders known in the darkness,
    or thy saving help in the land of forgetfulness?

O Lord, why dost thou cast me off?
    Why dost thou hide thy face from me?
                    (Psalm 88:10-12, 14)

The psalmist no doubt faced death as he had endured a diseased life— under the sense of divine forsakenness.

A final lament of the ill which we shall examine, Psalm 102, is a combination of lament elements interspersed with hymnic material. Much of this psalm suggests that it was or could have been used by the community as a congregational lament since it speaks of the restoration of Zion and of the descendants of the divine servants. The psalm opens with a cry for help (vv. 1-2), contains a description of distress addressed to God (vv. 3-11) and one addressed to the congregation (vv. 23-24), and finally has three hymnic praises of God, two addressed to the deity (vv. 12-14, 25-28) and the other, more confessional in tone, addressed to the congregation (vv. 15-22). Perhaps the lament was originally prayed by a community leader or spokesman.

The description of the distress speaks of the fever of illness (vv. 3-

5) which leads to isolation from the community (vv. 6-7) and to the taunt of enemies (v. 8). All is described as the work of God and as an expression of his indignation and anger (vv. 9-11, 23-24). Unlike Psalm 88, this lament looks upon the future with confidence, but it is a confidence in the future of the community. Zion will again be the recipient of divine pity; nations will come to fear the Lord; Jerusalem, as in the Zion psalms, will be a universal center of divine worship; and the children of God's servants will dwell secure.

LAMENTS OF THE ACCUSED

In a number of psalms, the worshiper pleads his case before God in terms which reflect a legal process. As was noted in chapter 1, Israelite legal practices took into consideration the fact that some charges brought against defendants could not be proven for lack of evidence or witnesses. When such charges were serious, such as those involving homicide, assault, and religious apostasy, special appeal to divine adjudication was resorted to. This involved certain rituals in the sanctuary in which the priests played a significant role (see Deuteronomy 17:8-13). First Kings 8:31-32 describes part of this ordeal in the following manner:

> If a man sins against his neighbor and is made to take an oath, and comes and swears his oath before thine altar in this house, then hear thou in heaven, and act, and judge thy servants, condemning the guilty by bringing his conduct upon his own head, and vindicating the righteous by rewarding him according to his righteousness.

Exactly how it was determined who was guilty and who righteous in cases involving such legal matters is not known. Such verdicts may have been decided by casting the sacred lots, by priestly observation of the parties, by divine signs associated with sacrifice, and so on. Deuteronomy 17:12 warns that "the man who acts presumptuously, by not obeying the priest who stands to minister there before the Lord your God, or the judge, that man shall die. . . ." Perhaps in some cases merely the act of declaring one's innocence in oath form was considered a self-fulfilling curse which would produce divinely ordained punishment in cases of guilt.

The so-called psalms of the accused are thus to be understood as prayers offered by accused individuals during these special rituals at the sanctuary. The clearest examples of these psalms of the accused are Psalms 7; 17; 26; and 27.

Psalm 7 opens with a statement that the worshiper has taken refuge in God and prays that he would be saved from his pursuers (vv. 1-2). Then he affirms his innocence before God and asks that if he has committed the act with which he is charged or wronged either friend or enemy he may be overtaken by his enemy and trampled in the dust (vv. 3-5). This conditional self-curse would thus constitute the oath sworn before the deity.

The worshiper pleads that God would vindicate him and arise in anger against the fury of his enemies (vv. 6-9). The role and function of God as judge and the importance of his verdict are stressed.

> . . . judge me, O Lord, according to my righteousness
> and according to the integrity that is in me.
>
> (Psalm 7:8)

Verses 10-11 are a confession of confidence not spoken to the deity but perhaps addressed to the priests, the opposing parties, or to friends and associates present.

> My shield is with God,
> who saves the upright in heart.
> God is a righteous judge,
> and a God who has indignation every day.

Following this confession of trust, verses 12-16 contain a declaration of the inevitability of judgment upon the wicked.

> [The wicked] makes a pit, digging it out,
> and falls into the hole which he has made.
> His mischief returns upon his own head,
> and on his own pate his violence descends.
>
> (Psalm 7:15-16)

The term "wicked" in this passage does not refer to a generally immoral man but denotes the guilty party in the conflict. Who was the speaker of this little poetic "sermon" on the inescapability of retribution? Probably the speaker was the priest who officiated over the arbitration and thus warned the defendant of the consequences of claiming innocence should he be guilty.

The psalm concludes, with the defendant as speaker, with a trustful vow to offer thanks and song to God (v. 17). The defendant could thus depart knowing himself, either through personal confidence or through divine-priestly verdict, to have been declared righteous, that is, the innocent, justified party.

Psalm 17 opens with a plea that God would attend to the worshiper's cry, to hear a just cause spoken by lips free from deceit. His hope is that vindication of his cause—the right—will come from God (vv. 1-2).

The accused admits to no wrongdoing but affirms that if God put him to the test at any time he would find no wickedness (vv. 3-5). Neither in word nor work does he transgress. By obedience to the divine commandments ("the word of thy lips"), he confesses he has avoided the ways of violent living. His feet have walked in the paths of God. Such a view of one's loyalty, fidelity, and innocence may strike us today as reflective of self-righteous conceit and as an overstatement of the person's purity. However, we must remember that the divine laws in ancient Israel were probably understood in their straightforward, literal sense. Once the laws were spiritualized, as they were by the prophets and Jesus, and were applied to attitudes as well as acts, innocence became a different matter.

The plea to God is contained in verses 6-9. The wicked and enemies, that is, his accusers, from whom he wishes to be saved, are described in verses 10-12. They are arrogant, pitiless, tracking down their prey like pursuing animals, raging like lions, waiting to see their victim cast to the ground.

Not only does the worshiper seek vindication for himself but he also prays for God to punish those who have falsely accused him (vv. 13-14). This is the counterpart to the cry for salvation in the double-appeal of the one lamenting—vindicate and save me and execute punishment upon my enemies. The psalm closes on a note of serene confidence.

As for me, I shall behold thy face in righteousness;
   when I awake, I shall be satisfied with beholding thy form.
                        (Psalm 17:15)

The worshiper is content in faith to rest his case upon the divine. The reference to "when I awake" suggests that in the morning worship service of sacrifice the accused will know vindication and will worship God (referred to in the metaphors "behold the face" and "behold the form") in righteousness and satisfaction, perhaps by offering a prayer and sacrifice of thanksgiving.

Psalm 26 begins with a plea to God that he would subject the accused to a thorough test and examination in order to vindicate him (vv. 1-3). The psalmist contends that he is willing to submit to thorough scrutiny, confident that before the divine he will stand vindicated and justified. Although it probably reads into the psalm more than was originally structured into it, the person's claims in his protestation of innocence can be seen as tenfold:

1. Walking in integrity (1*a*)
2. Trusting in the Lord (1*b*)
3. Remembering divine love (3*a*)
4. Walking in faithfulness (3*b*)
5. Not sitting with false men (probably idolaters) (4*a*)
6. Not consorting with dissemblers (probably members of some secret cult) (4*b*)
7. Hating evildoers (5*a*)
8. Not associating with the wicked (5*b*)
9. Proper worshiping of God (6-7)
10. Loving the temple (8)

Such a tenfold list recalls the tenfold requirements proclaimed for entrance into the temple given in Psalm 15.

The plea of the supplicant, found in verses 9-11, begs that he not be swept away with sinners, bloodthirsty men, schemers, and bribers.

The psalm concludes with a statement of confidence, "My foot stands on level ground," and a vow, "in the great congregation I will bless the Lord" (v. 12).

A psalm of lament in which the sense of confidence practically overshadows any feeling of distress is Psalm 27. The psalm opens with a lengthy assertion of great confidence not addressed to God but offered as a confessional statement (vv. 1-6). The speaker confesses that he has total reliance upon the Lord (v. 1) and has no need to fear though he were assaulted by enemies from his own community (v. 2) or attacked by some warring opponents (v. 3). Verse 4 which refers to dwelling in the house of the Lord, if not intended metaphorically, would suggest that this lament was offered by some temple functionary, though probably not by a priest since they did not live in the temple precincts. The priests at the Jerusalem temple only served during the festival celebrations and for two other weeks during the year on a rotation basis. Verse 10 implies that he may have been given to the temple by his parents. The praying individual expresses certainty that God will hide him from his enemies (v. 5) and that it will be he and not his opponents who will offer sacrifices of thanksgiving and shouts and songs of joy in the temple (v. 6).

The passage which points to some accusation as the basis of the man's distress is verse 12, which speaks of adversaries and false witnesses who have risen up against him. In his plea for help (vv.7-12) addressed to the deity, the psalmist reminds God that he has complied with the demand of God—he comes seeking the face of God and pleads that God not hide his face.

In verse 13, the speaker returns to his affirmation of confidence. He has faith that he will experience the goodness of the Lord as long as he lives. "In the land of the living" is a circumlocution to avoid making a reference either directly or indirectly to one's death when it was not imminent.

As we noted in discussing priestly instruction to the worshipers, verse 14 probably was a statement of encouragement spoken by a priest to the one offering the lament.

LAMENTS OF THE OPPRESSED

Numerous laments in the Psalter refer to foes, adversaries, and enemies who are harassing, persecuting, accusing, and oppressing the one offering the lament. Belonging to this group are Psalms 3; 9; 10; 13; 35; 52; 55; 56; 57; 62; 69; 70; 86; 109; 120; 139; 140; 141; and 143. Many of these psalms in style and content are similar to the laments of the accused, but some do not reflect and contain as clear legal terminology and practices as the psalms of the accused.

In attempting to understand these psalms, two questions immediately arise. Who is the persecuted and oppressed? Who are the enemies and the oppressors? Unfortunately neither of these questions can be answered with any certainty. Numerous suggestions have been made in attempts to identify the oppressed. Some scholars have suggested that the oppressed were the economically deprived and abused. The enemies would then be the wealthy and privileged. Frequently within these psalms the speaker does describe himself as poor, but how literally this should be taken is unsure. Others have seen the Israelite king as the oppressed. Under the onslaught of foreign enemies and armies, the king is the one who laments his status. This could apply to some of these psalms but not to all. The faithful pious have been proposed as the speakers. In such an interpretation, the enemies would be the wicked who sought to destroy the life and faith of the righteous. Without doubt, the ones lamenting in these psalms consider themselves righteous and their opponents wicked, but this is too general to offer much help in understanding. Some scholars have suggested that the oppressed in these psalms is actually the nation or whole congregation which personifies itself as an individual and thus speaks as an "I." The enemies would therefore be foreign states and powers out to oppress the Israelites. Many of these psalms could be so understood, but this probably does not supply the full answer. Finally, it has been proposed that the harassed are persons who considered themselves the object of magical spells and curses by workers of iniquity or sorcerers. As we noted earlier, some psalms may be so understood but certainly not all of the psalms which belong to this group.

Perhaps we should assume that these psalms were used under a wide variety of conditions and employed by different individuals, by the king and religious leaders and even on occasion by the nation as a whole. In the descriptions of both the enemies and the oppressed, we should assume that stylized, metaphorical designations are used which would be applicable to diverse circumstances. For example, when people describe their distress, they frequently borrow images from hunting, warfare, and communal and family strife to depict their conditions. Often, the descriptions are extremely general—"the whole world is against me!" Images and descriptions drawn from a wide range of distress situations can be employed to present one's dire circumstances. This means, however, that such descriptions cannot always be taken literally. No doubt this is the case with many of these psalms of the oppressed.

Because of the number of psalms of the oppressed, we shall not examine them in detail but simply note some of their dominant features and characteristic content.

In these psalms, the one lamenting does not offer any extended references to his person which would allow us to describe the person praying or the class to which he belonged. In Psalm 52:8, the speaker describes himself as "like a green olive tree in the house of God" who "trusts in the steadfast love of God for ever and ever." The opening of Psalm 86 illustrates how the worshiper describes himself as both poor and pious.

> Incline thy ear, O Lord, and answer me,
>   for I am poor and needy.
> Preserve my life, for I am godly;
>   save thy servant who trusts in thee.
> (Psalm 86:1-2*a*)

The destitute image projected by the one lamenting can be seen in Psalm 109:22-25.

> For I am poor and needy,
>   and my heart is stricken within me.

> I am gone, like a shadow at evening;
>   I am shaken off like a locust.
> My knees are weak through fasting;
>   my body has become gaunt.
> I am an object of scorn to my accusers;
>   when they see me, they wag their heads.

In Psalm 120:5-6, the speaker describes himself as a sojourner who lives far from the holy land among people who love war and hate peace.

A remarkable statement on God's omnipotent knowledge of the one praying is found in Psalm 139. The psalmist confesses that God has searched him and known him (v. 1). His sitting and rising, the paths he treads, and the words he speaks are all known by God who surrounds him (vv. 2-6). The worshiper affirms that there is no place to which he might flee which is beyond the care and concern of God—whether heaven, Sheol, the deep, or the darkness (vv. 7-12). He is known because it was God who created him and wrote the book of his life.

> For thou didst form my inward parts,
>   thou didst knit me together in my mother's womb. . . .
> Thou knowest me right well;
>   my frame was not hidden from thee,
> when I was being made in secret,
>   intricately wrought in the depths of the earth.
> Thy eyes beheld my unformed substance;
>   in thy book were written, every one of them,
> the days that were formed for me,
>   when as yet there was none of them.
>   (Psalm 139:13-16)

Instead of focusing on the person of the one presenting his condition before God, these psalms stress the situation of distress and the enemies who have produced such adversity. The portrayals of the dire circumstances range from very brief statements to long recitals of oppression.

> O Lord, how many are my foes!
>   Many are rising against me;
> many are saying of me,
>   there is no help for him in God.
>   (Psalm 3:1-2)

Malicious witnesses rise up;
    they ask me of things that I know not.
They requite me evil for good;
    my soul is forlorn.
But I, when they were sick—
    I wore sackcloth,
    I afflicted myself with fasting.
I prayed with head bowed on my bosom,
    as though I grieved for my friend or my brother;
I went about as one who laments his mother,
    bowed down and in mourning.
But at my stumbling they gathered in glee,
    they gathered together against me;
cripples whom I knew not
    slandered me without ceasing;
they impiously mocked more and more,
    gnashing at me with their teeth.
Let not those rejoice over me
    who are wrongfully my foes,
and let not those wink the eye
    who hate me without cause.
For they do not seek peace,
    but against those who are quiet in the land
    they conceive words of deceit.
They open wide their mouths against me;
    they say, "Aha, Aha!
    our eyes have seen it!"
                (Psalm 35:11-16, 19-21)

In the first of these passages (Psalm 3:1-2), the enemies are pictured as derisive individuals who declare the man beyond the help of God. In the second passage (35:11-16, 19-21), the opponents are community associates who seize upon the individual's disaster to become witnesses against him (in court cases?) and gossipers about his condition, seeking to swallow him up (35:25).

In Psalm 55, the enemy and oppressor is depicted as an old friend and acquaintance, which makes the situation even more lamentable.

It is not an enemy who taunts me—
    then I could bear it;
it is not an adversary who deals insolently with me—
    then I could hide from him.

> But it is you, my equal,
>   my companion, my familiar friend.
> We used to hold sweet converse together;
>   within God's house we walked in fellowship.
>   (Psalm 55:12-14)

In Psalm 10:2-11, the enemy is described as greedy for gain, as renouncing God and proclaiming atheism, prosperous, conceited, arrogant, deceitful, and lurking in ambush to seize the poor. In Psalm 52:1-7, in which imprecations are hurled at the foe, the enemy is described as mighty, plotting, loving evil, deceitful, and above all possessing a sharp, devouring tongue. Psalm 57:4, 6 speak of the enemy as devouring lions or as hunters who set traps for the oppressed. Psalm 109:2-5 describes the enemies as malicious gossipers and the distress as the work of their lying words.

> For wicked and deceitful mouths are opened against me,
>   speaking against me with lying tongues.
> They beset me with words of hate,
>   and attack me without cause.
> In return for my love they accuse me,
>   even as I make prayer for them.
> So they reward me evil for good,
>   and hatred for my love.

The plea for redemption in these psalms is primarily developed as prayers for the destruction or punishment of the enemies. A few of these laments, however, contain the type of appeals for salvation which we have seen previously—that is, they focus on the redemption from distress of the one praying.

> At an acceptable time, O God,
>   in the abundance of thy steadfast love answer me.
> With thy faithful help rescue me
>   from sinking in the mire;
> let me be delivered from my enemies
>   and from the deep waters.
> Let not the flood sweep over me,
>   or the deep swallow me up,
>   or the pit close its mouth over me.
>   (Psalm 69:13b-15)

Teach me thy way, O Lord,
  that I may walk in thy truth;
  unite my heart to fear thy name.

Turn to me and take pity on me;
  give thy strength to thy servant
  and save the son of thy handmaid.
                      (Psalm 86:11, 16)

Hide not thy face from me,
  lest I be like those who go down to the Pit.
Let me hear in the morning of thy steadfast love,
  for in thee I put my trust.
Teach me the way I should go,
  for to thee I lift up my soul.
Deliver me, O Lord, from my enemies!
  I have fled to thee for refuge!
Teach me to do thy will,
  for thou art my God!
Let thy good spirit lead me
  on a level path!
For thy name's sake, O Lord, preserve my life!
  In thy righteousness bring me out of trouble!
                    (Psalm 143:7*b*-11)

    A few of these psalms are rather subdued in their requests for God to bring calamity upon the adversaries and foes. However, the vast majority use vitriolic and caustic language in their prayers of revenge. In many, hatred for the opponent permeates every plea. If the enemies were understood as the sole cause of the lamenting one's troubles, then no redemption would have been possible without the suppression of these foes. One can understand why these pleas for the enemies' destruction are so severe. The punishment must be equal not only to the adversity suffered by the lamenting party but also equal to the enemies' real or imagined wishes and desires for the oppressed. Nonetheless, they still are a bit irritating to the nerve of modern sensibility. It should, however, be said that such stark prayers for revenge allowed the worshiper to give full expression to his feelings. Suppression of such feelings might have produced increased psychological problems. This full venting of the worshiper's hostility may have been something of a catharsis in and of itself. In addition, just as the person in distress probably on occasion depicted his condition in exaggerated metaphors, so might these pleas for the enemies' destruction represent overdrawn metaphors. Much cursing tends to overstate the true desires of the one cursing.

The plea for judgment on the enemy in Psalm 35 draws upon analogies from warfare, harvest, and travel to depict the hoped-for actions of the divine against the man's foes.

> Contend, O Lord, with those who contend with me;
>   fight against those who fight against me!
> Take hold of shield and buckler,
>   and rise for my help!
> Draw the spear and javelin
>   against my pursuers!
> Say to my soul,
>   "I am your deliverance!"
> Let them be put to shame and dishonor
>   who seek after my life!
> Let them be turned back and confounded
>   who devise evil against me!
> Let them be like chaff before the wind,
>   with the angel of the Lord driving them on!
> Let their way be dark and slippery,
>   with the angel of the Lord pursuing them!
>   (Psalm 35:1-6)

Occasionally the pleas against the enemy are expressed as retribution for his plots. In other words, the worshiper prays that what the enemy has plotted would befall him (see Psalms 56:5-7; 141:10). As a rule, however, the misery requested for the enemy seems to exceed what had been planned for the one lamenting.

Psalm 109 contains the harshest, strongest pleas for trouble upon the enemy. The psalmist calls down upon his enemy the whole gamut of human misery.

> Appoint a wicked man against him;
>   let an accuser bring him to trial.
> When he is tried, let him come forth guilty;
>   let his prayer be counted as sin!
> May his days be few;
>   may another seize his goods!
> May his children be fatherless,
>   and his wife a widow!

May his children wander about and beg;
  may they be driven out of the ruins they inhabit!
May the creditor seize all that he has;
  may strangers plunder the fruits of his toil!
Let there be none to extend kindness to him,
  nor any to pity his fatherless children!
May his posterity be cut off;
  may his name be blotted out in the second generation!
May the iniquity of his fathers be remembered before the Lord,
  and let not the sin of his mother be blotted out!
Let them be before the Lord continually;
  and may his memory be cut off from the earth!
For he did not remember to show kindness,
  but pursued the poor and needy
  and the brokenhearted to their death.
He loved to curse; let curses come on him!
  He did not like blessing; may it be far from him!
He clothed himself with cursing as his coat,
  may it soak into his body like water,
  like oil into his bones!
May it be like a garment which he wraps round him,
  like a belt with which he daily girds himself!
May this be the reward of my accusers from the Lord,
  of those who speak evil against my life! (Psalm 109:6-20)

Is it possible to understand such expressions of revenge as anything more than statements of deep and pure hatred? Two things should be noted in attempting to answer this question. In the first place, the requests plead that the enemy would be punished in the same manner as he had oppressed others. The prayer asks that the punishment equal the crime. Psalm 109:6-15 pleads that neither man nor God show kindness to the enemy and his family. Verse 16 explains why: he had never shown kindness! In verses 17-20, the appeal asks that what he had given or withheld be given or withheld from him. Secondly, it was a common practice when nations, and perhaps individuals, drew up treaties and agreements in the ancient Near East to seal these with curses which were to befall any violator of the agreement. These curses are very similar in content to the curses of this psalm. The psalmist then was probably borrowing from a stereotyped pattern and commonly used terminology in describing what he hoped would befall his opponent.

LAMENTS OF THE PENITENT

A number of the psalms which we have investigated have associated the troubles and adversity of the lamenting individual with his sin. Examples of this close association may be seen in Psalms 38:3-4, 17-20; 39:8-11; and 41:4. Sin and human calamity and troubles were thus frequently seen as interrelated phenomena in ancient Israel.

When a man sinned and sought atonement and forgiveness, he turned to the sanctuary and worship. Leviticus 4:1–6:7 and Numbers 5:5-10 discuss the procedures involved in making atonement for sin. Some of this material concerns rituals of atonement on behalf of the high priest, the whole congregation, and the ruler, but we are interested only in that material relating to the ordinary individual. The material in Leviticus 5 describes the actions associated with the offering of a sin sacrifice. Actions requiring a sin offering were sins committed unwittingly. Examples of these are failure to offer testimony at a trial which could result in the miscarriage of justice, contact with something unclean which rendered the individual unclean, or the uttering of a rash oath. To expiate the sin, the individual had to confess his sin and present an offering.

Leviticus 6:1-7 and Numbers 5:5-10 discuss actions which required guilt offerings. Examples of such sins are given: deceiving one's neighbor so as to make gain from him, robbery, oppression of the neighbor, or swearing falsely about property. In all of these cases, some injury to the neighbor has resulted. In such cases, the sinner was required, after being convicted, to restore to the injured party what had been taken from him plus one-fifth as restitution for the wrong. In addition, he had to confess the sin which he had committed and offer a sacrifice as a guilt offering to God. "And the priest shall make atonement for him before the Lord, and he shall be forgiven for any of the things which one may do and thereby become guilty" (Leviticus 6:7). The sins which are so described were considered "a breach of faith against the Lord" (Leviticus 6:1), that is, sins against one's neighbors were also sins against God. Since all laws in ancient Israel were seen as deriving from God, any breach of the laws was not only a criminal act but also an act of sin.

No doubt, psalms confessing sin and asking for forgiveness had a place within these rituals of atonement and especially in that part concerned with the confession of sin. Two Psalms, 25 and 51, provide examples of psalms which could have been utilized in such rituals.

Psalm 25 opens with an address to God (v. 1), a statement of trust (v. 2), and a plea that the speaker and others who wait for the

Lord should not be put to shame (v. 3). Then follows a plea that God would make known his ways and teach and lead the worshiper in divine truth (vv. 4-5). A plea for mercy and forgiveness asks that his transgression be forgotten.

> Be mindful of thy mercy, O Lord, and of thy steadfast love,
>   for they have been from of old.
> Remember not the sins of my youth, or my transgressions,
>   according to thy steadfast love remember me,
>   for thy goodness' sake, O Lord.
>
> (Psalm 25:6-7)

Next in the psalm appears three verses not addressed to the deity but proclaiming the ways of God with sinners. This was probably spoken by the officiating priest to the worshiper. To this the supplicant responds: "For thy name's sake, O Lord, pardon my guilt, for it is great" (v. 11). Verses 12-14 are again instruction, perhaps spoken by the priest. This section describes the man who fears the Lord and his fate. Verse 15 is a confessional statement, "My eyes are ever toward the Lord, for he will pluck my feet out of the net," probably addressed by the worshiper to the priest as a confession that he is one who "fears the Lord." The remainder of the psalm returns to the address to the deity, asking for gracious favor and the forgiveness of sin (vv. 16-22). The reference to the foes in verse 19 appears a bit abrupt in its context. Were these foes demons or powers which may have been considered the causes of the man's disobedience? In verse 21 he prays that integrity and uprightness would preserve him, perhaps seeing these (as personified protections?) as the counterbalance to the foes.

The classical lament of the sinful man in the Psalter is Psalm 51. It is the most penitential of all the psalms. The collectors and editors of the biblical psalms related its content and usage to David's attitude after the Bathsheba affair and David's orders to have her husband Uriah killed in battle (2 Samuel 11-12). Such an interpretation represents the collectors' attempts to understand some of the psalms as reflective of specific historical situations.

The psalm begins with a call to God for mercy and a cleansing from sin (vv. 1-2). In his confession of sin, the psalmist admits his transgressions and acknowledges the appropriateness of God's judgment.

> For I know my transgressions,
>   and my sin is ever before me.

> Against thee, thee only, have I sinned,
>   and done that which is evil in thy sight,
> so that thou art justified in thy sentence,
>   and blameless in thy judgment.
> Behold, I was brought forth in iniquity,
>   and in sin did my mother conceive me.
> (Psalm 51:3-5)

Two elements in this confession are especially noteworthy. (1) The psalmist sees his sin as a matter between himself and his God. The nature of his sin is not stated but it is understood as a disruption in the human-divine relationship. (2) The psalmist confesses that his entire life—his nature—is sinful in orientation. His life, from conception on, has been touched by sin and iniquity. One should probably not see in this any doctrine of inherited sin. The Hebrew Scriptures do not teach a doctrine of inherited sin, though they do argue that one generation could have visited upon it the penalties of the sins of an earlier generation (see Exodus 20:5, but compare Ezekiel 18:19-20).

In the psalmist's plea for deliverance from his sin (vv. 6-12), he does not pray merely for the forgiveness of sin. He asks that his entire life be renovated and transformed. In verse 6, "wisdom in my secret heart" is requested and since the heart was, for the Hebrews, the organ of the intellect and will, we could say he is asking for a transformation of character. Purgation and cleansing are the plea of verse 7. In much of the Old Testament, sin is presented as a contaminating stain or impurity whose removal is here requested. Hyssop was a small bush whose twigs were used in the cult to sprinkle sacrificial blood and purification waters. Verse 8 asks that the joy and gladness of life be restored. Verses 10-12 restate the requests of verses 6-8 with the exception that verse 11 requests the presence of God and his Holy Spirit.

Psalm 51:13-17 contains the vow of the lamenting petitioner. The vows we have noted earlier tended to stress sacrifice and praise of God in worship. Here the psalmist vows three things. (1) He will use his experience to teach other transgressors the divine will and to bring them into relationship with the deity (v. 13). (2) He will sing aloud in praise of God's redemption. This suggests thanksgiving in public worship (vv. 14-15). (3) He will serve God, not with sacrifice, but with a contrite heart and spirit submissive to the divine will (vv. 16-17). Verses 18-19 were probably added to the original psalm when it came to be used as a congregational song of penitence.

5

Psalms of Individual Thanksgiving

The counterpart to the lament, which looks out of distress and petitions for redemption, is the thanksgiving psalm, which looks back upon the alleviated distress and praises God for the experience of redemption. In the thanksgiving psalm, the adversity has either passed or else the worshiper possesses assurance that the distress will be overcome. As we noted earlier, many laments shift from petition to assurance, suggesting that some transformation in the psalmist's status could occur within the lament service.

THE STRUCTURE OF THE THANKSGIVING PSALM

As a rule, the thanksgiving psalms open with a call to give thanks or a reference to offering thanks: "I will extol thee, O Lord" (Psalm 30:1); "I love the Lord" (116:1). The second element, and generally the most fully developed, is the description of the distress from which the psalmist was delivered. Often this description makes reference to the appeal made to God out of the distress. A good example of this element is found in the psalm of thanksgiving in the Book of Jonah.

> "I called to the Lord, out of my distress,
>   and he answered me;
> out of the belly of Sheol I cried,
>   and thou didst hear my voice.
> For thou didst cast me into the deep,
>   into the heart of the seas,
>   and the flood was round about me;
> all thy waves and thy billows
>   passed over me.
> Then I said, 'I am cast out
>   from thy presence;

> how shall I again look
>   upon thy holy temple?'
> The waters closed in over me,
>   the deep was round about me;
> weeds were wrapped about my head
>   at the roots of the mountains.
> I went down to the land
>   whose bars closed upon me for ever;
> yet thou didst bring up my life from the Pit,
>   O Lord my God.
> When my soul fainted within me,
>   I remembered the Lord;
> and my prayer came to thee,
>   into thy holy temple."
>
> (Jonah 2:2-7)

As we noted in the psalm of distress, the person praying often made reference to vows which he would keep if he were rescued from his troubles. The psalms of thanksgiving frequently refer to the fulfillment of these vows.

> "But I with the voice of thanksgiving
>   will sacrifice to thee;
> what I have vowed I will pay."
>
> (Jonah 2:9)

Psalms of thanksgiving have a strong element of praise to God which frequently runs throughout the psalm. Sometimes it appears as a concluding affirmation: "Deliverance belongs to the Lord!" (Jonah 2:9).

THE USE OF THANKSGIVING PSALMS

Within the vows pledged by worshipers in the psalms of distress, there are frequent references to future acts of worship to be performed when the cause of the distress has disappeared. Psalm 7:17 contains the following vow:

> I will give to the Lord the thanks due to his righteousness,
>   and I will sing praise to the name of the Lord, the Most High.

In Psalm 9:14, the worshiper prays for God's deliverance so "that I may recount all thy praises, that in the gates of the daughter of Zion I may rejoice in thy deliverance." Psalm 26:12 declares, "in the great congregation I will bless the Lord." Psalm 52:9 states: "I will proclaim thy name, for it is good, in the presence of the godly." Psalm 54:6 speaks of the freewill offering to be sacrificed, and Psalm 56:12 refers to the presentation of thanksgiving. Psalm 71:15 has the speaker promise: "My mouth will tell of thy righteous acts, of thy deeds of salvation all the day." Such references made it clear that thanksgiving, sacrifice, praise, singing, recitation of God's redemptive acts, and rejoicing followed the alleviation of the distress and took place in public services in the sanctuaries. This setting as the locale for the thanksgiving psalms is further confirmed by statements in the thanksgiving psalms themselves.

> I will come into thy house with burnt offerings;
>   I will pay thee my vows,
> that which my lips uttered
>   and my mouth promised when I was in trouble.
> I will offer to thee burnt offerings of fatlings,
>   with the smoke of the sacrifice of rams;
> I will make an offering of bulls and goats.
>   (Psalm 66:13-15)

> What shall I render to the Lord
>   for all his bounty to me?
> I will lift up the cup of salvation
>   and call on the name of the Lord,
> I will pay my vows to the Lord
>   in the presence of all his people.
> I will offer to thee the sacrifice of thanksgiving
>   and call on the name of the Lord.
> I will pay my vows to the Lord
>   in the presence of all his people,
> in the courts of the house of the Lord,
>   in your midst, O Jerusalem.
>   (Psalm 116:12-14, 17-19)

This secondary service of sacrifice before God was required of persons who had been healed from certain contagious diseases. As we noted in chapter one, when an illness made one unclean, the individual, after healing, had to undergo purification rituals which reintegrated him into the community. A part of this ritual (Leviticus 14) involved the offering of sacrifice. One can easily see how some thanksgiving psalms could have been employed in this ritual of sacrifice which ended the long process by which the worshiper became "fully human" again and was restored to his place in family, community, and cult.

Thanksgiving psalms were also used in contexts where the thanksgiving was not just the response to redemption from a situation of distress. Thanksgiving could be and often was a response to the blessings bestowed upon a person by God. Generally, however, this thanksgiving and praise were celebrated in the community festivals. We shall examine this element in more detail in chapter 7. However, there were no doubt cases where individuals or small groups offered thanksgiving in the sanctuary, not because they had been redeemed from some calamity, but because they had enjoyed the benefits of divine blessings. The Mishnah, which discusses various practices and rituals in Judaism, provides one such example. When worshipers came to Jerusalem bringing their first fruits—a portion of their year's produce—they were met at the temple court by the Levites who sang Psalm 30—a thanksgiving psalm—on their behalf. (Many of the individual psalms may have been sung on behalf of the worshiper by the professional temple singers.) Then, repeating after the priest, the worshipers recited the confession of faith found in Deuteronomy 26:3-11.

THANKSGIVING FOR RECOVERY FROM ILLNESS

Several psalms of thanksgiving make reference to redemption from illness and were no doubt employed in thanksgiving rituals after a person had recovered from sickness. Among these are Psalms 30; 103; and 116.

In Psalm 30, the psalmist offers thanksgiving for healing.

> . . . thou hast drawn me up,
>   and hast not let my foes rejoice over me.
> O Lord my God, I cried to thee for help,
>   and thou hast healed me.
> O Lord, thou hast brought up my soul from Sheol,
>   restored me to life from among those gone down to the Pit.
>   (Psalm 30:1-3)

The psalmist here describes his healing in terms of having been rescued from Sheol and the Pit. But surely the man had not died and been resurrected! In other words, the references must not be taken literally. In many laments, the petitioner describes himself as brought down to Sheol, which must be understood as a reference to being near death. In many psalms, Sheol and death are presented almost as personified powers. A person who was sick or diseased was already under the power of death and Sheol which were slowly invading the individual's life, laying claim to that person.

Since the thanksgiving services were public events probably attended by friends and family, and since they involved testifying to God's salvation, much of the thanksgiving psalms are addressed, not to the deity, but to the congregation present. So the psalmist calls upon others to join in his praise and to learn from his experience.

> Sing praises to the Lord, O you his saints,
>   and give thanks to his holy name.
> For his anger is but for a moment,
>   and his favor is for a lifetime.
> Weeping may tarry for the night,
>   but joy comes with the morning.
>
>   (Psalm 30:4-5)

The psalmist then rehearses the prayer of lament which he offered previously (vv. 8-10) and concludes with thanksgiving.

> Thou hast turned for me my mourning into dancing;
>   thou hast loosed my sackcloth
>   and girded me with gladness,
> that my soul may praise thee and not be silent.
>
>   (Psalm 30:11-12*a*)

This passage illustrates the two moods of worship—mourning to dancing, sackcloth to gladness, lamenting to thanksgiving, and, although this passage contains no such reference, fasting to feasting since the thanksgiving offerings were mainly consumed by the worshipers.

Psalm 103 seems to be a thanksgiving psalm although it reflects many of the characteristics of the hymn. None of the psalm is in the form of direct address to God. This suggests, as was noted earlier, that many of the words of the thanksgiving service were addressed to the congregation. The importance of this instruction, proclamation, or preaching to the worshipers attending the service with the one offering thanksgiving is stressed in Psalm 40.

> I have told the glad news of deliverance
>   in the great congregation;
> lo, I have not restrained my lips,
>   as thou knowest, O Lord.

> I have not hid thy saving help within my heart,
> I have spoken of thy faithfulness and thy salvation;
> I have not concealed thy steadfast love and thy faithfulness
>   from the great congregation.
> (Psalm 40:9-10)

Psalm 103 opens with an address of the worshiper to his soul—to himself—to bless God who forgives iniquity, heals diseases, redeems from the Pit, crowns one with love and mercy, satisfies with good, and renews youth (vv. 1-5). These verses suggest that this psalm is thanksgiving for healing. Verses 6-14 are a theological proclamation on the saving activity of God and how his mercy leads not to punishment but forgiveness. The following passage is one of the greatest Old Testament comments on divine forgiveness:

> He does not deal with us according to our sins,
>   nor requite us according to our iniquities.
> For as the heavens are high above the earth,
>   so great is his steadfast love toward those who fear him;
> as far as the east is from the west,
>   so far does he remove our transgressions from us.
> As a father pities his children,
>   so the Lord pities those who fear him.
> For he knows our frame;
>   he remembers that we are dust.
> (Psalm 103:10-14)

Over against the transitory character of the individual human life—which grows, blossoms, and perishes—stands the mercy and steadfast love of God from generation to generation for those who fear him, keep his covenant, and obey his commandments (vv. 15-18). The psalm concludes with a call for the angelic powers and all creation to bless the Lord (vv. 19-22).

Psalm 116 opens with an affirmation of the psalmist's love for God because the divine has responded to his prayer and supplication (vv. 1-2). The opening words, in fact, almost the entire psalm, are addressed to the human audience. Perhaps we should envision the thanksgiving ritual as a complex of events and spoken words. Preliminaries probably involved proclamation to those attending, stressing the present status of the one offering thanks and reciting how he cried out in his distress and was heard and saved. Then, just prior to the offering of sacrifice, prayer and praise could have been offered by the worshiper in terms addressed directly to God.

Following the offering of sacrifice, the sacrifice would have been cooked and eaten by the worshiper and his associates in a meal celebrating his new status and rejoicing over his redemption (see the reference to dancing in Psalm 30:11). According to the sacrificial laws in Leviticus 7:11-15, the thanksgiving offering had to be cooked and eaten in its entirety on the day it was offered. Psalm 116 thus probably belonged to the preliminaries of the thanksgiving sacrificial ritual although there are two passages in the psalm addressed to God.

Verses 3-4 of Psalm 116 demonstrate that the psalm was offered by one who had recovered from sickness. His distress is described as having been encompassed by the snares of death and laid hold of by the pangs of Sheol. In other words, he was sick unto death. But God answered his plea and he now proclaims to the congregation the greatness of God and testifies to how God saved him (vv. 5-6). In verse 7, he addresses his troubled soul to assure himself that his distress has been dealt with. Verse 8 in the present form of the text is addressed to God and could thus represent an emotional outburst, a spontaneous little prayer. Verses 9-11 are a confession that the psalmist now walks in the ways of God and that when ill he always rested his faith in God and not man. References to the forthcoming fulfillment of his vows occur in two forms. In verses 12-15, 18-19, fulfillment is proclaimed to those in company with the worshiper. In verses 16-17, reference to the fulfillment occurs in a prayer to God.

OTHER THANKSGIVING PSALMS

The Psalter contains thanksgiving psalms which could have been used by individuals on occasions when they offered thanks other than for having been saved from sickness. Psalm 32 is a psalm of thanksgiving for the forgiveness of sin. The psalm opens with two blessings pronounced upon the man who is forgiven. In a temple ritual one can imagine these verses having been spoken by the priest in the service where the sinner gave thanks for his forgiveness. Verses 3-4, spoken to the deity by the worshiper, describe the distress which sin had brought upon the psalmist. When he confessed his sin, he experienced divine forgiveness (v. 5). In verses 6-7, the psalmist prays and in his prayer does a little preaching, asking that all godly men might offer prayer before they are overwhelmed in life, and he confesses that God is his hiding place. The remainder of the psalm, if one is unaware of what was happening in the service, sounds totally unassociated with what has preceded. It is instruction and admonition or, as we could say, preaching and a call to a way of life.

> I will instruct you and teach you
>   the way you should go;
>   I will counsel you with my eye upon you.
> Be not like a horse or a mule, without understanding,
>   which must be curbed with bit and bridle,
>   else it will not keep with you.
> Many are the pangs of the wicked;
>   but steadfast love surrounds him who trusts in the Lord.
> Be glad in the Lord, and rejoice, O righteous,
>   and shout for joy, all you upright in heart!
>   (Psalm 32:8-11)

What is happening here is that the one offering thanks addresses his audience directly, in proclamation and admonition. In other words, he is doing what the one lamenting in Psalm 51 promises he will do if he is forgiven: "I will teach transgressors thy ways, and sinners will return to thee" (Psalm 51:13).

Psalm 34 is a thanksgiving psalm which is dominated by the tone of proclamation and admonition. It is thus a parallel to Psalm 32:8-11. The references to redemption from distress only appear twice in the psalm and then in very general terms.

> I sought the Lord, and he answered me,
>   and delivered me from all my fears.

> This poor man cried, and the Lord heard him,
>   and saved him out of all his troubles.
>   (Psalm 34:4, 6)

Except for the opening call to worship (vv. 1-3), the psalm testifies to and proclaims the care and protection of God for the righteous and the contrite and the retribution which will befall the wicked and the evil. Many of the sayings in this psalm are very similar to passages one finds in the book of Proverbs, which reflects the common wisdom of the Israelites. This instruction would be, however, the type one would anticipate from the average Israelite who was neither priest nor prophet but who sought to instill in his friends and audience a fear and trust in God and who was seeking to get people to learn from his experience. Throughout the psalm, there are several calls for the hearers to trust God and follow his ways (see vv. 5, 8-9, 13-14). In verse 11, the psalmist addresses his hearers as a father addresses his sons or as a teacher addresses his students: "Come, O sons, listen to me, I will teach you the fear of the Lord." Many of the psalms which are primarily instructional in nature (see Psalms 1; 37; 112; 119; and 133) may have originally been used when the worshiper sought to instruct his hearers in the faith or when priests gave instruction to the worshipers.

Psalm 111 is a thanksgiving psalm whose primary content is a hymn of praise. That the psalm was used in a context of thanksgiving is indicated by verse 1: "I will give thanks to the Lord with my whole heart, in the company of the upright in the congregation." The psalm contains no reference to the distress from which the individual might have been saved nor to any special reason for offering thanks. That a thanksgiving psalm should take the form of a hymn of praise is not surprising. Frequent reference is made in the vows of the laments to offering praise to God after the passage of the distress (see Psalms 7:17; 9:14; 13:6; 35:28). Psalm 111 praises the great works and acts of God, especially the protection and care for Israel in the wilderness (v. 5) and the gift of the land of Canaan to his people (v. 6). The work of God's hands is declared to be faithful and just and his precepts trustworthy (vv. 7-8). The two-fold stress of verse 9 emphasizes the redemption of God and the commands of his covenant. Or we could say that the psalmist is claiming that in the redemptive acts of the past and in the commands of the covenant, a person possesses the means to study the ways of God (see vv. 2, 4) and such study should lead to the fear of God which is the beginning of wisdom (v. 10).

Ancient Israelites not only experienced crises which threatened their general well-being but they also experienced crises of faith. Psalm 73 can be understood as the thanksgiving psalm of one who had undergone a severe crisis of faith during which he was tempted to forsake his religious heritage.

> But as for me, my feet had almost stumbled,
>   my steps had well nigh slipped
> For I was envious of the arrogant,
>   when I saw the prosperity of the wicked.
>   (Psalm 73:2-3)

The man believed that "God is good to the upright, to those who are pure in heart" (v. 1), but he could not reconcile this with the status, wealth, and reputation of the wicked and irreligious. The arrogant and the wicked seemed to possess all the signs of success and divine blessing.

> For they have no pangs;
>   their bodies are sound and sleek.

> They are not in trouble as other men are;
>   they are not stricken like other men.
> Therefore pride is their necklace;
>   violence covers them as a garment.
> Their eyes swell out with fatness,
>   their hearts overflow with follies.
> They scoff and speak with malice;
>   loftily they threaten oppression.
> They set their mouths against the heavens,
>   and their tongue struts through the earth.
> Therefore the people turn and praise them;
>   and find no fault in them.
>   (Psalm 73:4-10)

Such success and status in spite of wickedness had led people to assume that God really took no knowledge of their lives (v. 11), in other words, that God was not in control of human life and he did not uphold justice in history. In light of the success of the arrogant and wicked, the psalmist was tempted to say that he had suffered and endured in his faith for nothing (vv. 14-15). Attempts to reconcile his fidelity to God and his misery in life with the infidelity of the wicked and their ease and riches in life had proven to be "a wearisome task" (v. 16). He was tempted to declare his religion irrelevant and erroneous. He was at the point of saying,

> All in vain have I kept my heart clean
> and washed my hands in innocence.
>   (Psalm 73:13)

The resolution of this conflict in his life (a conflict which has troubled people throughout history) and a satisfying answer came only when he went into the sanctuary of God and perceived their end (v. 17). The psalmist does not tell us what occurred in the sanctuary which gave him the means to conquer his conflict. Could he have heard and come to understand the type of instruction within the temple based on human experience which we have seen in Psalms 32 and 34?

The psalmist then offers to God a statement of his newfound condition. Previously, he says, "my soul was embittered, when I was pricked in heart, I was stupid and ignorant, I was like a beast toward thee" (vv. 21-22), but now he was informed and at peace with God. What had he learned and experienced in the sanctuary for which he now could praise God? He had come to understand that the status of the wicked and arrogant was only temporary.

> Truly thou dost set them in slippery places;
>> thou dost make them fall to ruin.
> How they are destroyed in a moment,
>> swept away utterly by terrors!
> They are like a dream when one awakes,
>> on awaking you despise their phantoms.

> For lo, those who are far from thee shall perish;
>> thou dost put an end to those who are false to thee.
>>   (Psalm 73:18-20, 27)

Had he seen in the sanctuary some arrogant and wicked man forced because of some distress to plead to God only to experience a divine word of rejection? One can only wonder.

Secondly, he had come to understand that in his faith in God and divine justice he experienced a nearness to God and a faith in the future which could not be shaken.

> . . . I am continually with thee;
>> thou dost hold my right hand.
> Thou dost guide me with thy counsel. . . .

> But for me it is good to be near God;
> I have made the Lord God my refuge,
>> that I may tell of all thy works.
>>   (Psalm 73:23-24a, 28)

> . . . afterward thou wilt receive me to glory.
> Whom have I in heaven but thee?
>> and there is nothing upon earth that I desire
>> besides thee.
> My flesh and my heart may fail,
>> but God is the strength of my heart and my portion
>> for ever.
>>   (Psalm 73:24b-26)

Does this last passage only refer to the psalmist's belief that nothing in life could separate him from God's presence and that if he possessed that, it was enough? Or does this passage already show a struggling belief in some hereafter where justice will prevail? Such a passage certainly did not discourage the developing belief in a meaningful existence beyond death in which fidelity would be rewarded.

Royal Psalms

6

A number of psalms within the Psalter were composed and used in services in which the king was the center of focus. These psalms can be isolated on the basis of their content. Insofar as type is concerned, the royal psalms encompass several of the psalm types which we have already examined. There are royal laments and thanksgivings but also special psalms probably employed in unique rituals associated with the king.

In ancient Israel, the king was far more than an ordinary individual who was assigned the task of national leadership. But unlike the ancient Egyptians, the Hebrews never considered their monarchs to be divine or an incarnation of deity. The kings who ruled in Jerusalem were all members of the family of David which was considered the elect, chosen dynasty. The king was understood as a son of God, having assumed this special status and relationship at the time of his coronation. Like most kings, Davidic rulers were leaders in warfare, in the economic and political life of the state, and in religion. They were also considered upholders of social order and justice and, in a special way, defenders of the poor, widowed, and orphaned—the dispossessed in the land. The beliefs and convictions about the king were the grounds upon which Jewish messianism was built. The messiah to come was expected to be the ideal ruler from the house of David who would fulfill the promises and hopes of an ideal future.

A number of occasions in Israelite life provided opportunity for the utilization of the royal psalms—the time of the coronation, rituals before the king went into battle and upon his return, royal weddings, illness or other major calamities, and periods of rejoicing over national or personal triumphs.

97

CORONATION PSALMS

No biblical text provides a full discussion of what went on when a new king assumed the throne in ancient Israel. Two texts (1 Kings 1 and 2 Kings 11) describe how two men became king during times of community turmoil. First Kings 1 narrates how Solomon gained the throne from his brother Adonijah who had himself proclaimed king before the death of David. Second Kings 11 tells how the boy king Joash was placed on the throne and how the queen Athaliah, who had usurped the rule by force, was removed and killed. From these texts we can deduce some of the actions and ritual of the coronation. The steps in the coronation ritual were the investiture, the anointment, the acclamation, and the enthronement. These various stages in the coronation can be seen in 2 Kings 11:12, 19: "Then he [the high priest Jehoiada] brought out the king's son, and put the crown upon him, and gave him the testimony; and they proclaimed him king, and anointed him; and they clapped their hands, and said, 'Long live the king!' . . . and they brought the king down from the house of the Lord, marching through the gate of the guards to the king's house. And he took his seat on the throne of the kings."

The coronation rituals were held in a sacred area—in the case of Solomon, at the Spring of Gihon, and in the case of Joash, in the Solomonic temple. The investiture consisted of placing the crown upon the king's head and presenting him with the testimony. The crown, of course, is an understandable item; however, the testimony is not so obvious. The identity of the testimony, solemnly presented to the new king, has been associated with the written document presented to the new pharaoh in Egypt upon his accession. This document, associated with a divine origin, spelled out the rights and conditions of the monarch's rule and also contained the new names or titles bestowed upon the king. The testimony is best understood as the Israelite counterpart to this Egyptian royal document. In 2 Kings 11, the priest is in charge of the investiture and the subsequent rites; however, in 1 Kings 1, the prophet Nathan is an important participant in the rituals. Perhaps we should think of priests and prophets—both officials of the cult—as playing significant roles in the entire coronation process.

The anointing of the king consisted of pouring sacred oil upon his head, perhaps a ritual setting him apart as sacred and endowed by the divine. The king thus became the "anointed one." Since the word for anointed one in Hebrew is *messiah,* the king became the messiah in the coronation and the Israelite king reigned as the messiah.

The acclamation of the people is referred to in the blowing of the trumpet, the clapping of hands, and the shout, "Long live the king!" (1 Kings 1:34; 2 Kings 11:12). The acclamation represented the people's acceptance of the new ruler, sort of an oath of allegiance, and allowed the participation of the general population in the coronation ceremonies.

The king was escorted to the royal palace where he took his seat upon the throne and thus assumed the role and authority bestowed upon him. At the accession of Joash, various covenants were made— between the king and God, the people and God, and the king and the people. Whether such covenant making and renewals were a routine feature of coronation rituals cannot be determined, since the 2 Kings 11 account is the only passage in which they appear. The special significance of the covenant making in the Joash story may be due to the nature of the occasion. A Davidic ruler was reassuming the throne in Jerusalem after an interruption of seven years, during which time the throne had been occupied by Athaliah, the usurper queen.

The coronation was a time of jubilant celebration by the community. The story of the coronations of Solomon and his rival brother refers to offering sacrifice, eating and drinking, playing on pipes, and rejoicing with great joy. "The earth was split by their noise" (1 Kings 1:40).

The royal psalms which can be understood within the context of the royal coronation are Psalms 2; 72; 101; and 110. These psalms give expression to the Israelite beliefs about the king and allow us to visualize the theology of kingship which underlay the monarchy. These psalms were no doubt employed at significant points within the coronation ceremony, but their exact setting cannot be determined.

Psalm 2 opens with a description of the nations conspiring against God and his anointed (messiah) in Zion (vv. 1-3). The nations and their kings who are depicted as plotting in conspiracy seem to be portrayed as vassals to the Jerusalem king. Verse 3 refers to the breaking of the bonds which had held them in subservience. If the psalm envisions actual nations, then perhaps we should think of such countries as Ammon, Edom, and Moab over whom David ruled. The nations, however, should probably be understood in symbolic terms. They represent the hostile powers—foreign countries—which posed a real or actual threat to the Judean state. We have already noted such symbolic descriptions of the enemies which threatened Jerusalem in the Zion psalms.

Verses 4-6 are a statement of assurance that God has no thought of allowing their plans to materialize. In fact, he laughs at their plans and holds their plotting in derision. Over against the conspiracy and plotting, God is said to react in wrath and fury. In response to the nations, God declares that in Zion, his holy hill, he has established his king. This passage affirms the two dominant beliefs about Jerusalem. Zion was God's sacred city and in Zion the chosen viceroy of God ruled in the person of the Davidic king.

Who spoke verses 1-6 in the royal ceremony is uncertain. Perhaps it was some cultic official, either a prophet or priest. With verse 7, the king becomes the speaker. The king summarizes, in verses 7-9, the promises and assurances granted to him by God. The decree referred to in verse 7 should probably be identified with the testimony given to the king and noted in the account of Joash's coronation (2 Kings 11:12).

The king's summary of the decree stresses two elements: the king's adoption as son of God and the promise of a universal rule over the nations of the world. The king became the son of God on the day of the coronation. Verse 7 provides us with the formula of adoption: "You are my son, today I have begotten you." The king was thus "reborn" as a son of God on the day of his coronation. As God's chosen ruler, he enjoyed the special status of sonship; God became his father in a way that could be claimed only by the ruling monarch in Jerusalem.

The time of birth was a time for naming. The king in Jerusalem may have been given, like the pharaohs in Egypt, a new throne name or titles to denote his new status. Several Old Testament kings had two names. Solomon, for example, was also known as Jedidiah ("beloved of the Lord") (2 Samuel 12:25) and King Zedekiah's name was Mattaniah before he became king (2 Kings 24:17). The practice of using throne names or titles was widespread in the ancient Near East. The practice, in a limited way, can still be seen in the case of Catholic popes and British royalty.

It has been suggested, with some plausibility, that the giving of throne names is the background of Isaiah 9:6-7. This passage refers to the birth of a child and the giving of a son upon whom the government would rest and who would sit upon the throne of David. The text also contains four names or titles which are bestowed upon the ruler. The prophet Isaiah may have composed this passage with reference to King Hezekiah who was highly respected by the writers of the Old Testament and was remembered as one of the most faithful of all the nation's kings.

For to us a child is born,
  to us a son is given;
and the government will be upon his shoulder,
  and his name will be called
"Wonderful Counselor, Mighty God,
  Everlasting Father, Prince of Peace."
Of the increase of his government and of peace
  there will be no end,
upon the throne of David, and over his kingdom,
  to establish it, and to uphold it
with justice and righteousness
  from this time forth and for evermore.
                                        (Isaiah 9:6-7)

The second element noted in the divine decree to the new king was the promise of universal rule over the nations (Psalm 2:8). Throughout the Near East, reigning monarchs claimed to rule over the entire earth. This royal court concept was also a part of Israelite faith as this psalm demonstrates. Psalm 2:9 promises the king that he will break the foreign nations with a rod of iron and dash them in pieces like a potter's vessel. It is entirely possible that this belief was acted out in the coronation ritual. The ancient Egyptians used pottery figurines and dishes to symbolize foreign enemies and threatening powers and would break these to symbolize their destruction. Behind such a practice lies the concept of sympathetic ritual. The execution of a symbolic act, so it is believed, helps produce, in actuality, the event symbolized. (Something comparable to this still prevails at Friday night pep rallies before Saturday football games.) The Davidic king may have given symbolic expression to the concept of his universal dominion by smashing, with an iron rod, pottery vessels identified with foreign nations.

The remainder of Psalm 2, verses 10-12, constitutes a speech by the king to the foreign rulers calling upon them to be submissive to the Lord. "Kissing the feet" was a sign of complete subjection. (The only identifiable representation of an Israelite king in Near Eastern art shows the Israelite king Jehu kissing the ground at the feet of the Assyrian King Shalmaneser III.)

Psalm 2 allows us to glimpse some of the tenets of faith connected with the Davidic king. Further elements in this Davidic theology can be seen in Psalm 89:19-37. Psalm 89 is not a coronation psalm but a royal lament, which we shall examine later. The psalm, however, refers to the covenant between David and God and portrays its content more fully than does Psalm 2. A number of elements in this passage are noteworthy. (1) David was promised that God's arm and hand would uphold him and strengthen him (v. 21). (2) His enemy would not outwit him, for God promises to crush his foes (vv. 22-23). (3) God's love and faithfulness to David are assured (v. 24). (4) The king's rule was to be universal, reaching from the sea to the rivers (v. 25). (5) David could address and call upon God as "Father" (v. 26). (6) Among the rulers of the world, David was to be the firstborn, that is, the favored, since the firstborn received a double share of the inheritance (v. 27). (7) The divine covenant between David and God would never be violated by God. Even though the Davidic line should transgress the laws of God and receive divine punishment, it would never cease, for it would endure as long as the sun (vv. 28-37).

Another royal psalm probably employed in the coronation ritual is Psalm 110, a very difficult psalm to translate and interpret. The psalm appears to contain two divine oracles addressed to the king (vv. 1 and 4) and two choral or congregational responses (vv. 2-3 and 5-7).

Psalm 110, like Psalm 2, stresses the dominance of the Davidic king over his enemies and foreign nations. The oracle addressed to the king in verse 1 assigns the monarch a position of prominence at the right hand of God. In such a position, the king reigns along with God over the affairs of men. Such a statement as "sitting at the right hand of God" raises the question of how this was understood. In Jerusalem, the royal palace and the temple were part of a large royal complex. God was enthroned as king over the cosmos in the holy of holies of the temple. The king upon his throne in the royal palace thus sat enthroned at the right hand of God.

The reference to the enemies being the footstool of the king is best understood in terms of the royal throne furniture. We have no description of the footstool used by Davidic kings but practically all the art of the ancient Near East shows the use of footstools. Among the royal furniture discovered in the tomb of the Egyptian Pharaoh Tutankhamen were two footstools with stylized representations of the traditional enemies of Egypt worked into the wood as inlay. Thus, when the pharaoh sat upon his throne, his enemies were his footstool. Such a concept surely lies behind the reference in Psalm 110:1.

Psalm 110:2-3 refers to the king's rule from Zion in the midst of his foes, supported freely by his subjects. The latter half of verse 3 seems to refer to the promise of youthful vitality for the king, but the full meaning of the metaphorical imagery eludes us.

The king, in verse 4, is declared to be a priest forever, after the order of Melchizedek. The figure of Melchizedek appears in one other Old Testament passage. In Genesis 14:18, he is described as the king of Salem (Jerusalem?) and as priest of God Most High. Abraham is shown presenting a tithe to this priest-king after having been blessed (Genesis 14:19-20). If Melchizedek was a member or the founder of a pre-Israelite dynasty that ruled in Jerusalem prior to David's capture of the city, then Psalm 110:4 would suggest that the Davidic kings were understood as the successors to this priestly-royal line of monarchs.

The remainder of Psalm 110 stresses the divine intervention of God on behalf of his chosen king and promises the monarch that he will subject nations to his rule and annihilate his enemies.

Psalm 72 is a prayer of petition on behalf of the Davidic ruler which is best understood as utilized within the coronation ritual. This psalm gives expression to not only the status of the king amid the external world of the nations but also to the aspirations and hopes of the people for their benefit through the rule of the king. In addition, the psalm stresses the internal function of the king within Hebrew society.

The psalm opens with a prayer that the king would be given justice and righteousness so that his rule would establish a proper social order which was both just and prosperous (vv. 1-4). The king is here presented as the guarantor of the social order responsible for the operation of justice in the community. As the defender of justice, the king bore a special obligation for the defense of the poor and needy against those who would oppress them.

The close association between the nation's well-being, health, and prosperity and the life and fate of the king appears throughout this psalm. Prayer is made for a long life for the king (v. 5) and for his reign to fall upon the nation like the showers and rain that fall upon the land, rejuvenating the crops (v. 6). Righteousness and peace, which are requested in verse 7, denote the existence of right conditions and the total well-being of the community.

The universal dominion of the Davidic ruler is the theme of verses 8-11. The mythological expressions "from sea to sea" and "from the River to the ends of the earth" are equivalent to saying the whole world. "The kings of Tarshish and of the isles" were the Mediterranean powers to the west, and Sheba and Seba were the spice- and incense-rich states of South Arabia to the east. Both mythological and historical-geographical references are employed to give comprehensive expression to the universality of the dominion claimed by the Davidic king. The plea to God was that the king would have universal dominion over nations which would be submissive to his rule and lavish in their payment of tribute.

The responsibility of the king to protect and defend the weak members of society is the theme of verses 12-14.

> For he delivers the needy when he calls,
>   the poor and him who has no helper.
> He has pity on the weak and the needy,
>   and saves the lives of the needy.
> From oppression and violence he redeems their life;
>   and precious is their blood in his sight.
>
>   (Psalm 72:12-14)

There were no laws in ancient Israel requiring the king to protect the rights of those members of society who were open to exploitation by the privileged, wealthy, and oppressive. In fact the Old Testament legal material dealing with the king is very limited. The only regulations are found in Deuteronomy 17:14-20. Nonetheless, the society placed the king under the moral obligation to defend the defenseless, to aid the needy, and to pity the weak. In fact, the prophets applied this moral imperative to the whole of Israelite society, demanding justice in social affairs as service to God (see Amos 5:10-15, 24; Isaiah 1:12-23). The treatment of the poor, the fatherless, the widows, and the needy was seen as the real test of a society's commitment to divine justice. When the prophet Jeremiah wished to condemn the wicked King Jehoiakim, he did so by pointing to his construction of a lavish palace at the expense of the rights of the common man. When he wished to praise the good works of the righteous King Josiah, he did so by noting that this king "judged the cause of the poor and needy" (Jeremiah 22:13-17).

Psalm 72 concludes (vv. 15-17) with pleas that during the king's reign the land would know abundance and its cities would blossom with men—that there would be fertility in field and family—and that his name would become so renowned throughout the world that people would use his name when they sought to bless one another. (Vv. 18-20 are not part of Psalm 72 but belong to the editorial conclusions to collections within the Psalter.)

A final psalm which was used by the king in his coronation contains the monarch's commitment to a way of life in line with the ways and demands of God. One might call Psalm 101 the king's oath of office or his charter of rule. Verses 1-2 speak of loyalty, justice, and the way that is blameless. Psalm 101:2*b*-8 enumerates the character of the king's pattern of rule. These promises made by the king are tenfold:

[1] I will walk with integrity of heart within my house;

[2] I will not set before my eyes anything that is base.

[3] I hate the work of those who fall away;
    it shall not cleave to me.

[4] Perverseness of heart shall be far from me;
    I will know nothing of evil.

[5] Him who slanders his neighbor secretly
    I will destroy.

[6] The man of haughty looks and arrogant heart
    I will not endure.

[7] I will look with favor on the faithful in the land,
    that they may dwell with me;

[8] he who walks in the way that is blameless
    shall minister to me.

[9] No man who practices deceit
    shall dwell in my house;
    no man who utters lies
    shall continue in my presence.

[10] Morning by morning I will destroy
    all the wicked in the land,
    cutting off all the evildoers
    from the city of the Lord.

(Psalm 101:2*b*-8)

The monarch thus assumes responsibility for his own honesty and integrity, promises to abhor those who are apostate, perverse, slanderous, and arrogant, pledges to support and rely upon those who are faithful and blameless, vows to purge the dishonest from government service, and swears to carry out faithfully his role as arbiter of justice.

The royal theology of ancient Israel indeed clothed the king with a purple robe—seeing him as son of God, ruling over a universal dominion at the right hand of God, and functioning as a source of blessing that extended even to the world of nature. But this understanding of the role of the king laid upon the shoulders of the ruler burdens requiring responsibility and obligation to establish justice and order in society, to live in integrity, and to defend the cause of the weak and helpless.

When ancient Israel projected this royal theology into the future, messianism in its true sense was born. The people looked forward to the one who would come, one who would fulfill these promises and one who would exercise his reign in true justice and with full responsibility (see Isaiah 11:1-9).

After Jerusalem fell in 586 B.C., the Jews no longer possessed a king, but they preserved these royal coronation psalms, no doubt singing them in anticipation of that future messiah who would be the new David.

ROYAL LAMENTS

The royal coronation and the celebration of the anniversaries of the coronation, if these existed, were not the only occasions in which the king was the central figure in worship. There were numerous occasions when this occurred. Psalm 72:15*b* says of worship concerning the king: "May prayer be made for him continually, and blessings invoked for him all the day!" The king, as ruler and representative of the people, was involved in a special way when the society was threatened. Like any other individual, the king underwent times of individual and personal crisis, and for the king these were even more critical than for the common man. Perhaps during these crises such individual psalms of lament as we have already discussed were spoken by him or on his behalf. However, there are a number of psalms which seem to have been especially composed and employed with reference to the king. Among these laments are Psalms 22; 28; 61; 63; 71; 89; and 144.

The clearest example of a royal lament is Psalm 89. The following is the outline of the psalm: introduction (vv. 1-4), hymn of praise (vv. 5-18), recitation of the Davidic-divine covenant (vv. 19-37), description of the distress (vv. 38-45), and the appeal for help (vv. 46-51). The occasion for this psalm was a humiliation of the Davidic ruler which appeared to cast doubt on God's fidelity to the promises and assurances of the divine covenant with the house of David.

The extensive hymn within the context of a lament is similar to the appearance of hymnic elements in some laments of the individual. However, in this lament the hymn is more developed and could almost be treated as an independent psalm. Praise of God as the prelude to a petition to God was common in ancient Akkadian psalms and may have been more frequently employed in Israelite worship than is now reflected in the Psalter. This hymn preserves two theological concepts which have survived in only fragmentary form in the Old Testament. God is described as the chief or supreme deity in a heavenly council of divine beings (see Psalm 82).

> For who in the skies can be compared to the Lord?
> Who among the heavenly beings is like the Lord,
> a God feared in the council of the holy ones,
> great and terrible above all that are round about him?
>
> (Psalm 89:6-7)

The background for such a concept lies in polytheistic religions in which there were many gods, generally with one god reigning as supreme. In later Jewish thought, these heavenly beings are understood as angels, subordinate to God. The second concept is the idea that creation took place in conjunction with the slaughter of a rebellious god—the dragon of chaos (see Psalm 74:12-17). The monster in this psalm is called Rahab, who personified the hostile sea over which creation was established.

> Thou dost rule the raging of the sea;
> when its waves rise, thou stillest them.
> Thou didst crush Rahab like a carcass,
> thou didst scatter thy enemies with thy mighty arm.
> The heavens are thine, the earth also is thine;
> the world and all that is in it, thou hast founded them.
>
> (Psalm 89:9-11)

In this lament, the divine promises of God to David and his successors are enumerated in a fuller form than anywhere in the Psalter. These we have discussed in the preceding section of this chapter.

Why does his lament contain the hymnic praise of God as creator of the world and the references to the divine covenant with David? These must be seen as the background to the complaint of the king to God about the treatment he has received at the hands of his enemies and as the foundation of the king's hope in his special appeal to God. God as creator of the world and as father to the Davidic ruler is requested to aid the king in his struggles with his historical enemies as God subdued and ruled over his cosmic enemies.

The description of the king's distress (vv. 38-45) takes the form of a complaint against God, who appears to have cast off his elect, turned his back on his chosen, and aided his enemies. One can see in this complaint the crisis of faith which develops when the course of history appears to repudiate the beliefs by which one lives.

> But now thou hast cast off and rejected,
>> thou art full of wrath against thy anointed.
> Thou hast renounced the covenant with thy servant;
>> thou hast defiled his crown in the dust.
> Thou hast breached all his walls;
>> thou hast laid his strongholds in ruins.
> All that pass by despoil him;
>> he has become the scorn of his neighbors.
> Thou hast exalted the right hand of his foes;
>> thou hast made all his enemies rejoice.
> Yea, thou hast turned back the edge of his sword,
>> and thou hast not made him stand in battle.
> Thou hast removed the scepter from his hand,
>> and cast his throne to the ground.
> Thou hast cut short the days of his youth;
>> thou hast covered him with shame.
>
>> (Psalm 89:38-45)

In describing the humiliation which the king has undergone, the real enemy is God himself! The activity of the enemies is not their independent action but the strange work of God himself. If one looks for the historical occasion behind this psalm, the Babylonian capture of Jerusalem and the subsequent deportation of King Jehoiachin in 597 B.C. (see 2 Kings 24:1-17) appear as the most likely candidate.

The appeal of the king (vv. 46-51) consists of a plea for God to act out of his love and faithfulness and to remember the promises sworn to David and the present humiliation of the reigning recipient of those promises.

Psalm 144 is a psalm of lament employed when the king was threatened by foreign powers, perhaps during times of warfare. The plea that he be rescued from the cruel sword and from the hand of aliens (v. 11) points to the national leader as the spokesman as does the more fully developed request for divine intervention against the enemies.

> Bow thy heavens, O Lord, and come down!
>> Touch the mountains that they smoke!
> Flash forth the lightning and scatter them,
>> send out thy arrows and rout them!
> Stretch forth thy hand from on high,
>> rescue me and deliver me from the many waters,
>> from the hand of aliens,

whose mouths speak lies,
and whose right hand is a right hand of falsehood.
(Psalm 144:5-8)

The concluding petition for idyllic conditions (vv. 12-14) has
been understood by many scholars as out of context. However, as
Psalm 72 illustrates, the fate of the people and that of the king were
closely joined together. Thus a request for the king's welfare was
simultaneously a petition for the prosperity and well-being of the
people over whom he ruled.

Psalm 22 is one of those psalms which could be understood as
either a lament of the individual or a royal lament. The structure of
the psalm is extremely complex, moving back and forth among
statements of confidence (vv. 3-5, 9-10), descriptions of the distress
(vv. 6-8, 12-18), pleas for deliverance (vv. 11, 19-21), pledging of vows
(vv. 22, 25-26), and proclamation (vv. 23-24, 27-31).

No other psalm possesses such metaphors of misery as Psalm 22.
The one praying describes himself as under attack by bulls, lions,
dogs, and a company of evildoers. His enemies scorn, mock, despise,
and ridicule him; they have pierced or hacked his hands and feet and
are ready to divide up his very clothes. He speaks of himself as a worm
and no man, as emaciated and weak, and as without hope and already
in the dust of death. Even God has forsaken him and refuses to
answer his incessant prayer and pleading (vv. 1-2).

In spite of the destitute conditions described, and one must allow
for metaphorical exaggeration, the psalm proclaims a faith in
ultimate deliverance and vindication (vv. 23-24, 27-31). Such
proclamation may suggest that the worshiper had received assurance
of help. The vows to be fulfilled include proclamation in the
congregation in the context, no doubt, of a thanksgiving ritual. The
reference in verse 26a to the poor ones who would eat and be satisfied
points to a lavish sacrificial offering of a type which the king could
make (see 2 Samuel 6, especially vv. 18-19).

ROYAL THANKSGIVING PSALMS

Three psalms (Psalms 18; 118; and 138) describe situations of
distress and subsequent redemption for which thanksgiving is offered
that can best be understood as employed by the king after triumphs in
military engagements.

As we noted in discussing the individual psalms of this type,
thanksgiving psalms reflect a complex of rituals. In these rituals,
proclamation to the community and prayer to God were dominant

features along with the sacrifice of thanksgiving. The psalms alternate between address to the congregation and to the deity.

Psalm 18, after a short address to God (v. 1), opens with a confessional proclamation of faith in God (vv. 2-3) which declares God to be a rock, a fortress, a deliverer, a shield, a horn of salvation, and a stronghold in numerous military images.

Verses 4-24 describe the distress of the king (vv. 4-5), his prayer of appeal to God (v. 6), the intervention of God on his behalf (vv. 7-19), and the righteous life of the king which warranted such divine action for his salvation (vv. 20-24). The characterization of the divine activity stresses its cosmic dimensions. The earth reeled and rocked, its foundations trembled, the mountains quaked, God breathed smoke and fire, the heavens bowed down (see Psalm 144:5-8), the Lord thundered in heaven and rained down hailstones and coals of fire, arrows and lightning flashed, the channels of the cosmic sea were exposed, and the foundations of the world were laid bare (vv. 7-15). Such a description, of course, transcends historical reality and draws upon the imagery of the divine appearance in thunderstorms (see Psalm 19). In the description of the distress, the adversity too is portrayed in dramatic form—encompassed by the cords and snares of death and Sheol and assailed by the torrents of perdition. As we noted earlier, the imagery used to describe the misery of the one lamenting was drawn in as radical and dramatic a form as possible. In Psalm 18, the imagery of divine intervention is similarly expressed (see Judges 5:4-5, 19-21 for a parallel). The psalm therefore narrates an episode in which the king won a military victory but a victory which is described in the first part of this psalm as the result of cosmic intervention. The psalms, after all, are poetic material and one expects poetic license.

In proclaiming his victory to the congregation, the king claims that God intervened to rescue him as a reward for his righteous life.

The Lord rewarded me according to my righteousness;
    according to the cleanness of my hands he recompensed me.
For I have kept the ways of the Lord,
    and have not wickedly departed from my God.
For all his ordinances were before me,
    and his statutes I did not put away from me.
I was blameless before him
    and I kept myself from guilt.
                              (Psalm 18:20-23)

With verse 25, direct prayer to God begins but is interrupted again with proclamation in verses 30-34. Verses 35-45 offer thanks to God for the military victory and thus this section constitutes a parallel to verses 4-19. In the direct prayer the references to divine intervention are far more subdued. Here, the one praying uses terminology much more reminiscent of actual warfare. Enemies are pursued, thrust through, destroyed, beaten into dust, and foreigners are subdued.

The psalm concludes with additional thanksgiving and proclamation. Verse 50 was probably sung by a choir as the communal climax to the royal thanksgiving.

Psalm 118 allows us to see some of the various elements that went to make up the thanksgiving ritual. These elements can best be seen in an outline of the psalm.

1. Summons to the community to offer thanksgiving (vv. 1-4)
2. Description of the distress and proclamation (vv. 5-18)
3. Request for entry into the temple (v. 19)
4. Priestly response to the request (v. 20; see Psalms 15 and 24)
5. Direct thanks to God (vv. 21-22)
6. Choral or communal song (vv. 23-24)
7. Communal prayer (v. 25)
8. Priestly blessing (vv. 26-27a)
9. Liturgical directive (v. 27b)
10. Prayer of thanks, probably in conjunction with the act of sacrifice (v. 28)
11. Renewed summons to offer thanks (v. 29)

This psalm can best be understood as the verbal element which accompanied the ritual of thanksgiving held when the king and his soldiers returned from victorious battle. Just such an episode is discussed in 1 Maccabees 5:1-54, although it is not to be identified with the victory spoken of in Psalm 118. In the Maccabees account, Judas and his brothers rescue fellow Jews from the districts surrounding Judaea. After completing their military exploits, "they went up to Mount Zion with gladness and joy, and offered burnt offerings, because not one of them had fallen before they returned in safety" (1 Maccabees 5:54).

Although Psalm 118 is, in a narrow sense, a thanksgiving by the leader of the community, it is also a thanksgiving of the community since the whole group present joined in the festivities. In postexilic Judaism this psalm was used as a communal thanksgiving being sung in the temple and in the home during the Passover celebrations.

A final royal thanksgiving is Psalm 138 which, however, speaks of the salvation of the endangered in very general terms. The thanksgiving character of the psalm is evidenced in the introductory statement about offering thanks (v. 1) and in the reference to the favorable response of God to the earlier plea of the supplicant (v. 3). The relationship of the psalm to the Israelite king is suggested by the reference to the king's knowing of the word of God (v. 4) and by the supplicant's delivery by the right hand of God from his enemies (v. 7). The psalm was offered in the court of the temple where the great altar of sacrifice stood (v. 2).

OTHER ROYAL PSALMS

In addition to coronation psalms, royal laments, and thanksgivings, the Psalter contains other royal psalms. These include psalms which had their setting in preparation for warfare (Psalms 20 and 21) and one which belonged to a royal wedding (Psalm 45).

In ancient Israel, as in practically all other Near Eastern countries, warfare was a sacred undertaking and was thus executed with appropriate rituals and precautions. Among the rituals preceding going to war were the offering of sacrifice and petitions (see ·1 Samuel 7:5-11; 13:8-12). Psalm 20 belonged within such a context.

Psalm 20 opens with a petitioning oracle addressed to the king, expressing hope that God would hear the pleas and petitions of the anointed and grant him help in his undertaking.

> The Lord answer you in the day of trouble!
>   The name of the God of Jacob protect you!
> May he send you help from the sanctuary,
>   and give you support from Zion!
> May he remember all your offerings,
>   and regard with favor your burnt sacrifices!
> May he grant you your heart's desire,
>   and fulfil all your plans!
> May we shout for joy over your victory,
>   and in the name of our God set up our banners!
> May the Lord fulfil all your petitions!
>   (Psalm 20:1-5)

Who addressed such a petition cannot be determined. Was it a priest or a prophet or a temple choir? Verse 5 would suggest some representative of the community. Perhaps some cultic official in conjunction with a choral group offered such a petition as the king prepared to offer sacrifices to secure the aid of God (see v. 3).

Beginning with verse 6, the psalm is no longer in the form of a petition but assumes the character of confidence and assurance.

> Now I know that the Lord will help his anointed;
>   he will answer him from his holy heaven
>   with mighty victories by his right hand.
>
> (Psalm 20:6)

Who would have spoken such a statement of confidence—the king, a priest, or a prophet? Whoever spoke had come to an assurance that God had responded favorably to the petitions accompanying sacrifice. Perhaps the priest had witnessed the ritual and seen in its execution a favorable omen from God. Or else the king had acquired this confidence and could thus testify with such positive assurance.

With verses 7-8, communal address again prevails and confesses that the community's trust lies not in the instruments of war but in God who can grant victory. This, however, should not be read to suggest that the king went into battle without his chariots and horses! The psalm concludes (v. 9) with a choral or communal petition on behalf of the king and his military undertaking.

When we come to Psalm 21, it is difficult to know whether this psalm originally belonged to the preparation for war or to the ritual utilized upon the return from battle. Verses 1-6 suggest that the king has been granted success, whereas verses 8-12 assume that the struggle is still in the future. One can assume that the first half of the psalm refers to past divine aid and the latter half to future undertakings. If this be the case, then this psalm would have belonged to the rituals preparatory to battle.

Psalm 21:1-6 is addressed to God as a thanksgiving on behalf of the divine blessings poured out upon the king. As such, these may simply refer to the promises and assurances granted the king in his assumption of the throne of David, but they may encompass more than that since they seem to refer to specific requests. These verses could have been spoken by the king himself or by some cultic official on his behalf. Verse 7 confesses, but not in direct address to the deity, that the king trusts in the Lord. Here one should envision the king as speaker.

Verses 8-12 of Psalm 21 are an oracle of assurance addressed directly to the king. As we noted in discussing the individual laments, such oracles were probably frequently given as the response to petitions. The king is promised that 'he will find his enemies, turn them into a blazing oven, destroy their offspring and children, and put them to flight. The enemies' schemes and plans will be frustrated and God will fight against the enemies. The psalm concludes (v. 13) with a hymnic praise addressed to God.

Psalm 45 is a wedding song composed by some court poet (see v. 1) and sung to glorify the reigning monarch (vv. 2-9) and his bride (vv. 10-15). The psalm concludes with a statement to the king which promises him great and famous progeny (vv. 16-17). This psalm represents the only psalm in the Psalter sung in praise of the king. Ordinarily, in Israel, weddings were secular events. This may not have been the case, however, with royal weddings. The psalm allows us some insight into the opulence of the royal court and a glimpse at some of the flattery of the king which must have characterized court life.

Although the poet praises and flatters the king, he may also have engaged in some "preaching" to the monarch by making frequent reference to the king's responsibilities. The ruler is described as the fairest of men, one blessed with grace. The king, gloriously garbed in regal splendor with girded sword, can be visualized in the imagery of verse 3. The king is portrayed as the defender of the right and the cause of truth, whose arrows destroy his enemies. The throne of the king is proclaimed as eternal and his rule as one of equity and righteousness. The status and well-being of the king are reflected in the perfumes which scent his royal robes, in the ivory palaces where he is entertained by instrumental music, in the daughters of royalty that inhabit his mansion, and in the golden splendor of his queen.

The bride is addressed and admonished to forget her family and country (Tyre) and to give her affection and attention to her new husband. The bride in her wedding finery and her attendants and ladies-in-waiting are described being led in procession to the palace of the king.

The psalm concludes, like many modern Near Eastern weddings, with a statement expressing the hope and assurance of numerous offspring. Since fertility—numerous offspring—was considered a blessing from God (see Psalm 127:3-5), such a promise or blessing was especially appropriate for the king whose offspring would share in the rule of the Davidic dynasty to whom God had promised eternal rulership.

Communal Psalms

7

In a number of psalms, both laments and thanksgiving, the concerns are those of the community at large. The distresses and disasters experienced and the benefits and blessings enjoyed are those in which the whole people are involved. Such psalms can be isolated from personal and royal psalms and can be understood against the background of communal experiences.

As has been previously noted, many of the so-called individual and royal psalms in which an "I" speaks may have been used by the whole community as the need arose. A clear example of this personification of the community—or its reference to itself in the first-person singular—is Psalm 129. This psalm begins:

> "Sorely have they afflicted me from my youth,"
>   let Israel now say—
> "Sorely have they afflicted me from my youth,
>   yet they have not prevailed against me."
>
> (Psalm 129:1-2)

Here is an obvious case in which the community speaks of itself with the use of the first-person pronoun.

In this section, we shall limit our discussion to psalms that are unmistakably focused on communal concerns.

THE USE OF CONGREGATIONAL PSALMS

The major festival seasons were the primary times of worship in ancient Israel. These festivals marked the significant periods throughout the year. The importance and character of these festivals, as well as some of the psalms which had their setting in these celebrations, have been discussed in chapters 1 and 2.

The festivals were routine, scheduled times of worship. However, these were not the only occasions when the people assembled to express their sentiments and needs. Times of national adversity and distress warranted special services both during and after the calamity. Defeats in war, droughts and famine in nature, and pestilence and plague could bring out the community to plead its case and to seek redemption from God. Likewise, when the danger was past, thanksgiving and praise were in order.

The prayer attributed to Solomon in 1 Kings 8 refers to those occasions of social calamity when prayer was offered to God.

"When thy people are defeated before the enemy. . . . When heaven is shut up and there is no rain. . . . If there is famine in the land, if there is pestilence or blight or mildew or locust or caterpillar; if their enemy besieges them in any of their cities; whatever plague, whatever sickness there is . . ." (1 Kings 8:33-37).

This passage notes that under such situations the people could turn from their sin, acknowledge the name of God, and pray and make supplication to God in the temple.

Other biblical texts speak of the various acts associated with the offering of supplication to God (see Joshua 7:6-9; Judges 20:23, 26; 1 Samuel 7:5-11; Ezra 9:1-5; Nehemiah 9:1-2; Jeremiah 14:2; and Joel 1:8-2:17). These passages refer to the proclamation of a fast signaled by the blowing of trumpets, fasting, the wearing of sackcloth, weeping, wailing, mourning, lamenting, tearing of the clothes, coating the head with dust and ashes, pronouncement of judgment upon the people, offering of sacrifice, and praying to God. Such actions had a two-fold purpose: (1) to solicit the mercy of God and entice him to alleviate the condition and (2) to demonstrate the sorrowful, calamitous, and repentant attitude of the people.

The lamenting of the people and their offering of supplication are frequently connected with the sins of the people and their confession of transgressions against the demands of God. It should be remembered that Israel set aside a special day in the year for the annual expression of confession and guilt. This was the great day of atonement which was observed in conjunction with the autumn festival cycle (see Leviticus 16). In the priestly regulations concerning the rituals of this day, two aspects are prominent. First of all, special burnt offerings were sacrificed to make atonement for the sins of the whole community. Secondly, the sins of the people were confessed over the head of a specially selected goat which was then led into the desert and released. This goat symbolically carried away the sins of the people and enacted their purification. The day of atonement was observed on a routine basis and was not associated with any severe or unusual calamity.

The rituals of the day of atonement and special services of fast and supplication demonstrate that ancient Israel was willing to see herself in need of divine forgiveness even when life was proceeding in an ordinary fashion. She was willing and able to confront the problem of national guilt and to do so publicly. Such services required an actual confrontation with the problem of sin and wrongdoing. She acknowledged that her people must as a social unit accept the responsibility demanded by God, admit failures and shortcomings, and rely upon and accept the forgiving mercy of God. Such an approach to the problem of communal and social evil and sin expresses a healthy attitude. It frees the community from any exaggerated sense of social self-righteousness and constantly reminds the people that disobedience, wrong, and guilt have a powerful social and communal dimension. In addition, such rituals have a purifying effect upon the community which allows it to undergo the experience of catharsis. Confession of wrong and enactment of the rituals of forgiveness bring guilt into the open and deal with it in a therapeutic manner. Such institutionalization of the confession of guilt and the experience of forgiveness obviously possess the potential for becoming a mechanical process. However, it should be recognized that such a method of dealing with communal guilt is far superior to having no method at all for encountering the problem of national evil and guilt.

Because of the significance of Jerusalem and the temple in the life of the people, special fast days commemorated the trauma and significance of the destruction of the city and temple by the Babylonians in 586 B.C. The prophet Zechariah refers to four fasts which remembered this event (Zechariah 7:1-7; 8:18-19). These four fasts recalled the time when the siege of Jerusalem began, the day when the city fortifications were breached (2 Kings 25:1-4), the burning of the temple (2 Kings 25:8-9), and the later murder of the governor, Gedaliah, who had been appointed by the Babylonians (2 Kings 25:25).

The communal laments of the Psalter must be seen within the context of these routine and special services of supplication.

We possess few indications of the nature of thanksgiving services in ancient Israel. References are made to the singing of hymns and celebrations following victory over enemies (see Exodus 14:30–15:21; Judges 5; 1 Maccabees 4:24; 5:54; 13:51; 2 Maccabees 10:7, 38). But beyond this, little can be determined. This absence of references to special thanksgiving services may be explained in several ways. (1) The great festivals of Passover, Feast of Weeks, and Feast of Tabernacles were strongly oriented toward thanksgiving and praise and allowed the community opportunity to express such sentiments. (2) Situations of distress are always considered more as crisis situations requiring worship than situations following alleviation of adversity. (3) Thanksgiving rituals may have been far more spontaneous and less institutionalized than supplication rituals. At any rate, one must assume that such rituals were observed.

CONGREGATIONAL LAMENTS

In structure, communal laments contain the same basic elements as individual laments: address to God, description of the distress, and pleas for divine intervention. In communal laments, however, the vows are not given as important a place as in many individual laments.

In communal laments the anxiety, humiliation, pain, and suffering are those of the community. They frequently manifest the crises of faith which communal life underwent when the community found itself subjected to the sorrows and hurts of human existence and to the tyranny of history. Communal laments within the Psalter include Psalms 12; 44; 58; 60; 74; 79; 80; 83; 90; and 137.

Among these psalms, the greatest number are concerned with the national calamities and disasters which resulted from warfare and battle. Located between the great powers of Mesopotamia to the north and Egypt to the south and constantly threatened by hostile and marauding tribes and states from the desert to the east, Palestine in the ancient world seldom enjoyed very lengthy periods of peace.

Psalm 83 provides an example of a communal supplication offered prior to the military engagement. Since it is a prayer offered before any experience of disaster, the psalm can more correctly be called a petition rather than a lament. The psalm describes a coalition of forces which have entered a treaty agreement and conspired together to dispose of Israel (vv. 2-8). "They say, 'Come, let us wipe them out as a nation; let the name of Israel be remembered no more!'" (v. 4). The enemies of the nation are the neighbors of Israel aided by the strong Mesopotamian power of Assyria.

The petition in verses 9-18 requests that God would deal with these opponents in the same fashion as he had dealt with Israel's enemies of the past (vv. 9-12). Verses 13-18 make the hoped-for treatment more specific:

> . . . make them like whirling dust,
>   like chaff before the wind.
> As fire consumes the forest,
>   as the flame sets the mountains ablaze,
> so do thou pursue them with thy tempest
>   and terrify them with thy hurricane!
> Fill their faces with shame,
>   that they may seek thy name, O Lord.
> Let them be put to shame and dismayed for ever;
>   let them perish in disgrace.
> Let them know that thou alone,
>   whose name is the Lord,
>   art the Most High over all the earth.

In several of the communal laments, the nation has suffered a humiliating defeat in battle and out of the trauma of that experience appeals to God. Psalm 44 is an example. The psalm opens with a hymnic statement which reminds God of the great victories which he had granted Israel in the past (vv. 1-3), victories which were God's work.

> For not by their own sword did they win the land,
>   nor did their own arm give them victory;
> but thy right hand, and thy arm,
>   and the light of thy countenance;
>   for thou didst delight in them.
>
> (Psalm 44:3)

The psalm continues with confessional statements indicating that faith still sees God as the source of victory (vv. 4-8). In these verses, the leader or king speaks (vv. 4, 6) as well as the community (vv. 5, 7-8).

The description of the distress (vv. 9-16) consists of a series of complaints and accusations against God. If God is the one who grants victory, then he is also the one who has humiliated Israel. God is the enemy! He has cast off Israel, refused to support her in battle, made her flee from her enemies, given her wealth as spoil to the enemy, slaughtered her soldiers like sheep, scattered her people among the nations, sold them into slavery for a trifle, made them and the king a disgrace and a laughingstock among the peoples.

The community protests its innocence and denies that it deserves the treatment it has received from God (vv. 17-22). Denying that it is guilty of religious wrongs (vv. 17*a*, 18*a*) or moral infractions (vv. 17*b*, 18*b*) or idolatrous practices (vv. 20-21), the community can only see God as the source of its miseries.

The psalm concludes with a series of questions and imperatives which plead and demand that God rouse himself from his sleep—his carefree, unconcerned, and derelict attitude (vv. 23-26).

No other psalm shows such an accusatory attitude toward the divine. There is no polite piety or pretense in its words. But there is bitter resentment, gnawing doubt, and more than a tinge of anguish. Israel was unashamed of direct confrontation with God, of dialogue with the diety, of bringing her deepest emotions into the rhetoric of address to the divine. Maybe, at times, this was the only way the community could preserve its faith and perhaps its sanity. But after the accusations have been uttered and the imperative pleas spoken, the community does not fall back upon its innocence and righteousness but casts itself upon divine mercy: "Deliver us for the sake of thy steadfast love!" (Psalm 44:26).

A more subdued lament is Psalm 80, although it still attributes the national fate to divine activity. Two images are employed to understand the divine-nation relationship. These are the shepherd-sheep and farmer-vineyard analogies, although it is only the latter which is developed. Israel describes herself as a grapevine brought out of Egypt and transplanted in the land of Canaan. There the vine prospered and grew until the vineyard keeper, God, turned his back upon the field and tore down its enclosure walls, exposing it to the ravages of wild beasts (vv. 8-13).

The appeal of the community embodies three requests: (1) that God would look again with favor upon his vine, (2) that the enemies who have carried out the destructive work of God would perish, and (3) that God would uphold the king (vv. 14-17). The vow in verse 18 pledges fidelity and worship if God will only respond. The psalm concludes with a restatement of the choral or community refrain (vv. 3, 7, 19).

As we noted in examining individual and royal laments, an oracle of promise or assurance was often addressed to the supplicant as a response to the worshiper's plea. Psalm 60 provides a lament containing a divine oracle addressed to the community (see also 2

Chronicles 20:5-17). The psalm opens with a complaint against God for his actions against his people (vv. 1-4). Verse 5 pleads with God that he would deliver his beloved and grant victory. Then follows a divine oracle perhaps spoken by some cultic official.

> God has spoken in his sanctuary:
> "With exultation I will divide up Shechem
> and portion out the Vale of Succoth.
> Gilead is mine; Manasseh is mine;
> Ephraim is my helmet;
> Judah is my scepter.
> Moab is my washbasin;
> upon Edom I cast my shoe;
> over Philistia I shout in triumph."
>
> (Psalm 60:6-8)

The nations and geographical areas referred to in this divine speech were all either parts of the holy land or adjacent countries. Thus the oracle has God claiming his supreme control over the area, with which he can do as he likes. Who speaks in verse 9 is unclear. Perhaps it was the king, engaged with his people in a war against Edom. Verse 10 is again a complaint to God and verse 11 a plea for divine help. The psalm concludes with a confession of confidence (v. 12).

Two communal laments are concerned with the desecration of the temple by foreign forces. These are Psalms 74 and 79. Psalm 74 opens with a cry to God for help which complains of his treatment of the people, pleads for remembrance, and calls upon God "to see for himself" how the sanctuary on Mount Zion lies in ruins (vv. 1-3). Verses 4-11 depict the enemies' destruction and burning of the temple and plead with God to act, reminding him that the desecrators of his temple are his foes.

A hymn of praise (vv. 12-17) separates the description of the distress from the extended appeal for help. This hymn, like those associated with the autumn festival, praises God as the creator-king of the universe. It preserves the primitive concept of the creation of the world as the result of divine combat with dragons, in this case with Leviathan, the multiheaded monster. This creation faith formed the basis of the community's belief that God could act to alleviate the situation of distress. As creator of the world, God possessed the power and control to change the life and reverse the fate of Israel.

The psalms demonstrate the two-fold foundation of Israel's faith in God's activity—he was creator and controller of the world, as in this psalm, and he was the redeemer who had acted in history, rescuing his people from Egypt, guiding them in the wilderness, giving them the Promised Land, and protecting them from their enemies (see for example Psalms 44:1-3; 78; 83:9-12). Creation and history undergirded faith in God who made the world and brought into being a unique people.

Psalm 74 concludes with an appeal to God to remember his covenant with his people and to defend his name and honor in the world (see vv. 18-23).

Psalm 74 stresses the enemy's destruction of the Jerusalem temple. Psalm 79, which comes out of the same situation, centers on the suffering of the people and notes the ruin of the temple only in passing.

> O God, the heathen have come into thy inheritance;
>   they have defiled thy holy temple;
>   they have laid Jerusalem in ruins.
> They have given the bodies of thy servants
>   to the birds of the air for food,
>   the flesh of thy saints to the beasts of the earth.
> They have poured out their blood like water
>   round about Jerusalem,
>   and there was none to bury them.
> We have become a taunt to our neighbors,
>   mocked and derided by those round about us.
>
> (Psalm 79:1-4)

The people orientation of this psalm, unlike Psalm 74, leads to the communal confession of sin and to pleas for forgiveness (vv. 8-9). The appeal to God, however, does not neglect the request for the punishment of the perpetrators of the horrible suffering (vv. 6-7, 10-12). The psalm concludes with a vow to offer thanks forever (v. 13) if God will "return sevenfold into the bosom of our neighbors the taunts with which they have taunted thee, O Lord!" (v. 12).

Like the fall of Jerusalem, the Exile in Babylon seared itself into the conscience and psyche of Judaism. Although the impact of the Exile can be seen in much of the Old Testament literature, there are few references to it in the psalms. Psalm 137, however, does recall the experiences of the Exile—the despair, the taunting, the sense of being severed from Jerusalem, the symbol of sacredness, and the consuming thirst for vengeance. The significance of Jerusalem as symbol and source of yearning can be seen in verses 5-6:

If I forget you, O Jerusalem,
    let my right hand wither!
Let my tongue cleave to the roof of my mouth,
    if I do not remember you,
    if I do not set Jerusalem
    above my highest joy!

The Babylonians, because they burned Jerusalem and the temple, and the Edomites, because they fought against Jerusalem though they were considered kinsmen of Israel through Esau the brother of Jacob, personified the powers of evil and represented the embodiment of Israel's enemies. The harshest condemnations in the Old Testament were hurled against these two nations. This psalm gives us a taste of this animosity.

Remember, O Lord, against the Edomites
    the day of Jerusalem,
how they said, "Rase it! Rase it!
    Down to its foundations!"
O daughter of Babylon, you devastator!
    Happy shall be he who requites you
    with what you have done to us!
Happy shall be he who takes your little ones
    and dashes them against the rock!
                    (Psalm 137:7-9)

Such a statement goes beyond the wish to see one's enemies destroyed. It proclaims as blessed the one who is the instrument of vengeance.

A communal lament with interests different from those we have discussed is Psalm 90. This psalm opens with a hymn of praise which declares the eternity of God over against the transience of man (vv. 1-6). The distress of the people is due, first, to their sense of sin and the experience of divine wrath (vv. 7-8) and, second, to the brevity and sorrow of human existence (vv. 9-10). All of this is compounded because the people neither take due regard of divine wrath nor properly number their days so that they may gain a heart of wisdom (vv. 11-12).

The appeal to God requests that God would have pity and grant to the worshipers a sense of satisfaction, joy, gladness, and an understanding of the work of God (vv. 13-17).

If we attempt to locate a context within which this lament with its confessional tone was employed, there appears no better option than the day of atonement—the great day for confession and purification from sin. The psalm appeals for deliverance from sin and the meaninglessness of life and associates these with an immediate time reference. Such feelings would have been expected in the ritual of the day of atonement. "Satisfy us in the morning with thy steadfast love, that we may rejoice and be glad all our days" (v. 14).

CONGREGATIONAL THANKSGIVINGS

The laments, both individual and communal, greatly outnumber the thanksgiving psalms in the Psalter. This should not, however, be taken to mean that thanksgiving played an insignificant role in Israel. The hymns sung in everyday sacrificial services and those employed at the great festivals praised God for who he was and what he had done, and praise is a means of expressing thankful sentiments. Thankfulness was thus built into the structure of Israel's routine worship to a greater extent than lamenting and mourning.

Those psalms which can be designated as communal thanksgiving are Psalms 65; 66; 67; 75; 100; 105; 106; 107; and 124. Those elements which we have seen as basic to the individual psalms of thanksgiving reappear in congregational thanksgiving. Thanksgiving to God and proclamation to the people are important factors in these congregational psalms just as in the individual psalms of thanksgiving. Some of the communal thanksgivings begin with plural references ("we," "us") but shift to the first person ("I," "me"). This shift could be due to the poetical personification of the nation as a person, to the fact that the king or leader in worship spoke on behalf of the whole people, or to the fact that when thanksgiving sacrifices were presented, even on communal occasions, they were presented as individual offerings.

Psalms 65 and 67 are thanksgivings for abundance in nature and a good harvest and thus may have been employed during spring and fall harvest seasons. Psalm 65 emphasizes God's gracious visiting of the earth which he has created and sustained. God is praised for watering the earth with showers, for providing grain. His activity clothes the pastures and meadows with growth and flocks and the valleys and hills are decked with grain and shout and sing for joy. Psalm 67 proclaims that God has blessed his people and caused the world to yield its increase.

Perhaps the best known and most widely used psalm is Psalm 100 which in reality is not a full thanksgiving psalm but only a call to thanksgiving. The reasons stated in the psalm for offering thanksgiving rest upon God's activity in creation (v. 3) and his love experienced in history (v. 5).

Psalm 66, like Psalm 118, suggests an extended liturgy of thanksgiving. The psalm opens with a lengthy call to praise and thanksgiving addressed to all the land or earth (vv. 1-9). This is followed by communal thanks addressed directly to God (vv. 10-12). Interestingly enough, this section praises God for having subjected the people to testing and affliction. In verses 13-15, the speaker, either the community participating as individuals or the king as communal representative, denotes the acts of sacrifice as the fulfillment of vows promised during time of trouble. In verses 16-20, the speaker no longer addresses God but speaks to the worshiping community who is called to hear and learn from the experience of the celebrant. In other words, the passage is a testimonial bearing witness to the efficacy of prayer and to the assurance that one can rely upon the divine.

This testimonial to divine care and protection forms the entire content of Psalm 124. This psalm speaks of the distress from which the community was redeemed in very general terms, using metaphors drawn from flood terminology and hunting. The opening verse suggests that such testimonials were repeated in worship with the congregation reciting the words after the leader.

Psalm 107, after a general call to thanksgiving (vv. 1-3), enumerates various disasters from which people were delivered. These include those who were guided through desert wastes (vv. 4-9), those redeemed from prison (vv. 10-16), those healed from sickness (vv. 17-22), and those endangered at sea (vv. 23-32). The people who had experienced such redemption are called upon to offer sacrifices of thanksgiving, to sing of God's redemptive acts, to extol God in the congregation, and to praise him in the assembly of elders (vv. 22, 32). The psalm concludes with a hymn praising God for his bountiful care (vv. 33-42) and with a call to give heed and learn from such experiences (v. 43). One can imagine this psalm being used when Jerusalem was visited at festival times by throngs who wanted to offer special thanks in addition to participating in the general festival celebrations.

Just as Psalms 65 and 67 praise and thank God for his special acts in the world of nature, so Psalm 105 calls upon the community to offer thanks for God's gracious acts in history which brought Israel into existence. The history that is summarized begins with the Israelite patriarchs—Abraham, Isaac, and Jacob—and concludes with the gift of the Promised Land. It was in these events of sacred history that Israel saw her origin and the expression of God's election.

Two psalms, Psalms 75 and 106, in spite of their introductory call to give thanks (Psalms 75:1; 106:1-3), do not immediately give the impression of being thanksgivings. Psalm 106 appears to be the reverse side of Psalm 105. The latter narrates the great acts of God in Israel's history while the former narrates the stubbornness and perversity of Israel and the judgments of God upon his own people. Episode after episode in Psalm 106 is detailed to show how rebellious and sinful was Israel's history. How could such a psalm be considered the means to "give thanks to the Lord" (Psalm 106:1)? Perhaps a story in Joshua 7 will allow us to understand this a bit. In this passage, a man named Achan was guilty of stealing booty from the field of battle and thus of breaking a divine taboo. Joshua confronts the man: "My son, give glory to the Lord God of Israel, and render praise to him; and tell me now what you have done; do not hide it from me" (Joshua 7:19). Achan then confesses his sin. In this story, confession of sin is understood as a way of praising God and giving him glory. Such confession was a way of glorifying God by accepting his judgment— something for which one should be thankful (see Psalm 66:10-12).

Psalm 75 further illustrates the theme of judgment and thanksgiving. The psalm opens with a call to offer thanks (v. 1). This is then followed by a divine oracle spoken as a word of God (vv. 2-5) which has God assuring the community that he will function as judge and admonish the wicked and boastful. Verses 6-10 are a confession that it is God who executes judgment and administers the foaming cup of judgment.

The individual and community that can confess sin and accept judgment as the means to praise and glorify God—as a means of thanksgiving—have indeed journeyed far in the pilgrimage of life.

Index of Psalms
Discussed in the Text